Ancient
GREEK
Holidays

Ancient GREEK Holidays

Mab Borden

The Witches' Almanac
Providence, Rhode Island

Address all inquiries and information to
THE WITCHES' ALMANAC, LTD.
P.O. Box 25239
Providence, RI 02905-7700

Softcover:
13-ISBN: 978-1-938918-97-1
eBook
978-1-881098-29-4

First Printing February 2024

Printed in USA

1 2 3 4 5 6 7 8 9 10

Phoebus, of you even the swan sings with clear voice to the beating of his wings, as he alights upon the bank by the eddying river Peneus; and of you the sweet-tongued minstrel, holding his high-pitched lyre, always sings both first and last.

—tr. Hugh Evelyn-White

Table of Contents

Introduction   9

Gregorian Festival Dates   1

Festivals

Hekatombaion   25
     Aphrodisia
     Kronia
     Panathenaia
     Gymnopaidia

Metageitnion   39
     Karneia
     Metageitnia
     Heraklea

Boedromion   49
     Genesia
     Charisteria for Artemis Agrotera
     Eleusinian Mysteries

Pyanepsion   69
     Proerosia
     Pyanepsia
     Theseia
     Oschophoria
     Stenia and Thesmophoria
     Apaturia
     Chalkeia

Maimakterion   91
     Pompaia

Poseideon   97
     Sacrifice to the Winds
     Haloa
     Country Dionysia

Gamelion   107
   Lenaia
   Gamelia

Anthisterion   115
   Anthesteria
   Lesser Mysteries
   Diasia

Elaphebolion   127
   Elaphebolia
   Asclepieia
   City Dionysia

Munichion   137
   Festival of Eros
   Procession to the Delphinion
   Munichia
   Olympieia

Thargelion   149
   Thargelia
   Bendidia
   Kallynteria and Plynteria

Skiraphorion   161
   Arrephoria
   Skira
   Dipolieia
   Diisoteria

Periodic Festivals and Festivals of Uncertain Date   173
   Pan-Hellenic Games
   Daidala
   Hyacinthia
   Festival of Pan

Appendices   187

Festivals by Deity Name   188
Appendix of Lunar Month Dates   196

Bibliography   198

Introduction

To call any calendar or cycle of festivals "Ancient Greek" is necessarily a misnomer. It would be more accurate to call them a calendar or festivals from ancient Greece, or to be more specific and call festivals specifically Athenian, Spartan, Delphic, etc. Ancient Greece was not a politically unified region and represents a broad time period, representing the long era between Neolithic settlement and 146 BCE, or from the ninth to the second centuries BCE, depending on which scholar you're asking. By either measurement, it's a very long period. Physically, Ancient Greece generally refers to the Aegean islands and the area surrounding the Aegean Sea, bounded to the South by Crete and including both modern Greece and the modern Turkish coast as well, since that area was populated by Greek-speaking people of Greek cultural origin until just before World War I.

CALENDARS

While there are lunar month names in Mycenaean Linear B tablets, there are only seasonal references in Homer, with no months mentioned. Greek city states had calendars that differed from one another in the month names and specific festivals and festival dates, but they shared a pattern of 12 months, alternating between "full" months of 30 days and "hollow" months of 29 days. Because the solar year is longer than twelve lunar months but shorter than thirteen, each city state had its own system of inserting extra days or months to reconcile the lunar and solar patterns to keep the calendar from drifting too much. In Athens, every few years—without pattern—an additional month would be added to the calendar to account for the differences between lunar and solar years.

Ancient Greek calendars are somewhat solar, somewhat lunar, and mostly civic. There is more than one type of calendar—in Athens alone you can calculate by Olympiad (a set of four years,) by the prytany calendar (a 10-month civil calendar) or by the lunisolar festival calendar. The agricultural and military rhythms are less dominant than in other ancient calendars. There was also an agricultural calendar with references as early as in Hesiod's Works and Days in the 8th century BCE. It referred to celestial events such as the rising of stars as guidelines for planting, harvesting, etc. Greece is very hot and dry, and the agricultural seasons begin much earlier than is common in Northern Europe and most of North America. That calendar was akin to a modern farmer's almanac and is not used to determine the timing of holidays, as the festivals mark the cycles of civic life more than the cycles of nature.

The majority of festivals presented here are Attic, not because Athens is more important than the rest of Greece but simply because it's the information that is available after more than two millenia. There is considerably more surviving evidence about the calendars and festivals of Athens and her surrounding territory—Attica—than about any other city state. For this reason, the month names used here are Attic and the year is set to begin in July with the month of Hecatombaion. The festivals of other cities have been incorporated as much as possible, with a few given at the end where the date is unclear. The only religious festivals which can be called truly Panhellenic are the series of Games that occurred at intervals of years rather than on an annual basis, and these are also discussed at the end.

Ancient Greek days began at sunset, and the Athenian year began with the sighting of the first New Moon after the Summer Solstice. Months ideally began on the New Moon, however the lunar and civil months did not line up perfectly and dates of holidays were determined by the civil calendar. This is convenient for the modern Pagan, as mapping a 12-month ancient civil year onto a modern 12-month modern year removes the need to reconcile the modern calendar with the lunar months. This book trades ancient month names for modern, without attempting to follow a lunar pattern. Ancient festivals were civic occasions which were not particularly tied to the cycle of the seasons, with a few exceptions. However, if you desire to celebrate these festivals by their lunar dates, you can calculate them by taking the date provided as that number of days after the New Moon that falls in that month. For example, the festival of Genesia falls on the 5th day of the month of Boedromion. You can celebrate this on September 5th, on the 5th day after the New Moon in September or on the 5th day after the third New Moon in the year, beginning with the first New Moon after the Summer Solstice. The beginning date of each lunar month through 2030 is provided in the appendix. The lunar year is eleven days shorter than the solar year. To avoid seasonal drift, you will need to insert an extra month every three years.

As the months drifted in ancient times, though, celebrating a festival a little earlier or later is of little consequence. Many festivals are only loosely tied to the time of year, but for those that have a significant seasonal aspect you can also time them at the appropriate seasons in your own geographic region. You might, for example, shift the Anthesteria—a festival involving the first flowers—from February to April if that is when they bloom in your area. Because modern hunting seasons are strictly legislated, you could honor Artemis the Huntress for Elaphebolia at the beginning or end of your local deer hunting season if you personally are a hunter. If not, it might make more sense to offer her stag-shaped cakes on the traditional date.

The most important practice for the lunar month was a household ritual, rather than a state-run festival. The Deipnon (dinner) for Hekate and the spirits happened on the last night of the month. All debts should be paid and business taken care of to avoid carrying the loose threads of the old month into the new. Then the house would be cleaned and fumigated, and the floor sweepings, the censor, any leftover parts of sacrifices or incense ash from the household altar, as well as food offerings set at the crossroads for Hekate and the spirits of the newly dead, after which no members of the household would leave the home. It was widely acknowledged in ancient times that the food offerings were consumed by the very poor. The following day was the Noumenia, the first day of the lunar month, when the first sliver of the moon was visible. Offerings of incense, cakes and flowers were given to the household Gods, particularly Hekate and Hermes, who were guardians of the household. In Athens, the guardians of the city received these offerings on the Acropolis as part of the state cult.

In the Athenian calendar, the first few days of each month are reserved for specific Gods. The first day was the Noumenia and the second day of the month was a day to offer and tend to the agathos daimon—the protector spirit of the household. The third was for Athena because she was born on the 3rd and the fourth was for Heracles, Hermes, Aphrodite and Eros. Days 6 and 7 were for the birthdays of Artemis and Apollon respectively (Gods' birthdays are monthly occasions) and the 8th day was for Poseidon and Theseus.

Because this book is concerned with holidays specifically, the focus is on the city-wide festivals rather than the home-based lunar practices. However, household worship is arguably the backbone of modern Hellenic polytheism, and any reader interested in engaging more deeply and personally with the Gods of Olympus is encouraged to seek out Hellenic reconstructionist groups for guidance in establishing a household practice in addition to festival-based worship.

SACRIFICE

As mentioned above, sacrifice—(thusia)—is the heart of ancient Greek ritual practice. Sacrifice is petition, supplication and prayer. Archaeologists have turned up a huge number of votive offerings at temple complexes and other religious sites, but these play less of a role in festivals. Animals were offered most frequently, but cakes and other non-animal foods were also given to the Gods. It is important to note that most sacrifices were food offerings and these were shared by the people attending a festival, which served as a community unifying event, being part block party as well as religious rite.

The standard pattern of sacrificial offerings can be seen in the works of Homer. First there was a procession to the temenos (sacred precinct) of the particular God. This may or may not include a temple. If there was a temple, it was the house of the God, not the site of worship, and the temple typically served as the backdrop for the sacrifice which took place at an open air altar. The procession was often long, accompanied by music and included people carrying the various implements required for the rite, as well as the animals needed for the sacrifice. Participants washed their hands to purify themselves, then took handfuls of barley from a basket. The animal was made to nod to consent to its coming death and then participants threw their barley grains onto the altar. The animal was then killed by cutting the throat. Sometimes it was stunned with a blow to the head first and a bit of the animal's hair was cut off and offered first. Women called out at the moment of slaughter and the blood was poured on the altar. The thigh bones were wrapped in the fat on the animal and burned on the altar as the Gods' portion. Other portions of meat could be offered to the Gods as well or placed on or near their statues. The rest of the meat was cooked and consumed by the community. Modern Hellenists typically process, wash their hands, throw barley, offer some food to the Gods and share some of it themselves.

A recurring theme in Greek literature is the practice of human sacrifice, which is consistently represented as barbaric, ancient and horrifying. It represents the other, the non-Greek and the aberrant. The Greeks thought of themselves as civilized and others as generally less so, to greater and lesser degrees depending on the culture. The rejection of human sacrifice is one way that they reminded themselves of this identity. While the modern reader might find the idea of animal sacrifice itself barbaric, to the Greeks it represented a round rejection of barbarism. Anyone wishing to honor the Greek Gods should feel comfortable offering any ordinary food item, including pre-prepared meat. It is not more holy to slaughter it on the altar, and given modern sensibilities, it is perhaps less so. The Gods will be just as pleased and there is plenty of ancient precedent. Pythagoreans embraced vegetarianism from the late 6th century BCE onwards and there is evidence at least in Athens of the poorer citizens offering cakes shaped like animals in lieu of the animals themselves.

PRIESTHOODS

Ancient Greek priesthoods were often inherited, purchased or appointed politically. They were not full-time jobs and the priest might attend a God in the temple as few as ten days per month. Some priesthoods functioned primarily at specific festivals. Typically, Goddesses were served by priestesses and Gods by priests, but there were significant exceptions to this, particularly in the Eleusinian Mysteries. Although some specific roles required associated ornaments, the priests wore ordinary clothing rather than any sort of religious vestments at most ritual occasions. Again, the Mysteries are an important exception. Generally, priests would wear garlands, as would everyone else at festivals.

While the priesthoods were not significant economic occupations, they came with honors and perks, such as seats at the theatric performances at the City Dionysia. Priests were treated with respect and were entitled to receive certain portions of sacrifices. The service of a priest was not strictly required for a sacrifice. Individuals, families and groups could and did offer sacrifices on their own, maintaining the same general ritual structure of washing, throwing barley and killing an animal, pouring libations or offering food.

A NOTE ON RECONSTRUCTIONISM AND PLURALISM

This series of books on ancient holidays is intended to inform the modern Pagan by offering reliable historical information. Empowered by this information and inspired by the Gods, you are free to incorporate as many or as few of these holidays into your own personal, family or group pagan practice as you see fit, in whatever ways you deem appropriate. Without the existence for most people of actual temple complexes to the Olympian Gods in their regions, some adaptation will be necessary. While acquiring barley to throw on the altar is as simple as making a trip to the grocery store, some aspects of the ancient rituals—such as throwing dead piglets in caves and then retrieving the remains months later—will be nearly impossible to recreate and the important thing to focus on will be the spirit of the rite. That particular festival is about fertilizing the fields, so establishing a more conventional compost pile in honor of Demeter would be a perfectly fine substitute. As long as it is done with respect for the deities and the ancient traditions, there is no reason to be concerned that you don't actually have an Acropolis nearby, that you are not inclined to kill a goat or that you might also worship other Gods.

That last is particularly important. The ancient polytheisms were additive. Ancient Egyptian Holidays demonstrated how the many different creation myths of Egypt were stacked one upon another to add meaning like building colors in an egg tempera painting. The apparent narrative conflicts were not conflicts at all, but enrichment. This is true between cultures as well. The ancient world was much more cosmopolitan than many modern people imagine and there was contact between cultures. Isis was worshiped in Greece, Cybele in Rome. The Roman empire is a prime example because the Romans found parallels between their own Gods and those of the polytheistic peoples they fought and (usually) conquered, but they weren't overly concerned with making it all fit neatly. Whatever the local worship was, they just wanted an extra sacrifice added to the Gods who protected Rome (and, of course, taxes.) But if you already believe there are many Gods, there's no conflict in believing there are a few more than you previously assumed. The Greek Gods are not jealous and they have never asked their worshippers to only believe in or only worship Greek Gods. The modern Pagan's experience of thunder can be simultaneously hearing Zeus and Thor because both control the lightning. Any apparent conflict is merely superficial and the ancient myths seem to revel in these sort of paradoxical ideas. After all, if you can believe that Heimdall had nine mothers, surely you can believe that the sea is ruled by Poseidon, Triton, Njord and Yemaya without conflict between them.

It is perfectly reasonable to celebrate Demeter in the Thesmophoria in October, Samhain at the end of the month and then begin the festival of Khoiak for Osiris a few days later. It might become incoherent to attempt to blend them and the reader is advised to respect the ancient Gods as they are. That does not mean you can't honor and practice across pantheons, though, and the most important thing, however you use the information in these books, is to proceed in a spirit of worship and celebration.

Gregorian Festival Dates

The dates below are based on mapping the ancient months directly onto the modern, beginning by placing Hecatombaion in July. Festival dates can also be calculated based on the number of days after the New Moon in each month using the method described in the introduction. The beginning dates of each month are listed in the appendix through 2030.

July 4: Aphrodisia, an Athenian festival of Aphrodite

July 12: Kronia, the Athenian celebration of a festival for Kronos

July 16: Synoikia, an Athenian holiday to celebrate the union of the towns and peoples of Attica under Athens

July 17 and 18: The celebrations of the Orgeones in Athens, in honor of their Gods

July 28: Panathenaia, a major festival of Athena in Athens

July, date uncertain: Gymnopaidia, a Spartan festival honoring Apollon

August 7–15: Karneia, a Spartan festival in honor of Apollon

August 15–18: Eleusinia, an Athenian festival distinct from the Eleusinian mysteries

August 16: a sacrifice to Kourotrophos, Hekate and Artemis from Erchia

August 19: a sacrifice to the Heroines from Erchia

August 20: a sacrifice to Hera Telchinia from the town of Erchia

August 25: a sacrifice to Zeus Epoptes from Erchia

August, date uncertain: Metageitnia, an Attic festival for Apollon

August, date uncertain: a festival for Herakles in the Attic town Kynosarges

September 4: a sacrifice to Basile by the Attic town of Erchia

September 5: Genesia, an Athenian feast of the dead

September 6: Charisteria, an Athenian sacrifice of thanksgiving to Artemis Agrotera

September 12: Democratia in Athens

September 15–20: Eleusinian Mysteries in Attica

September 18: Epidauria, an Attic festival for Asclepius on the 4th day of the Mysteries

September 25: Boedromia, an Athenian feast of thanksgiving to Apollon

September 27: a sacrifice to Athena by the Attic town of Teithras

September 27: a sacrifice to the nymphs, Achelous, Alochus, Hermes and Gaia by Erchia

October 5: Proerosia, a tithe to Demeter in Eleusis

October 7: Pyanepsia, a festival in Eleusis for Pythian Apollon

October 8: Theseia, an Athenian festival in honor of the hero Theseus

October 8: Oscophoria, an Attic winemaking festival in honor of Dionysus

October 9: Stenia, a minor Athenian festival for Demeter and Persephone

October 11–13: Thesmophoria, an Athenian women's festival for Demeter

October 14: a sacrifice to the Heroines by the Attic town of Erchia

October 19–21: Apaturia, a festival for the phratrai

October 30: Chalkeia, an Athenian festival for Athena and Hephaestus

November, date uncertain: Maimakteria, a possible feast for Zeus of Blustering Storms

November, date uncertain: Pompaia, a purification rite of Zeus Meilichios

December 5: Plerosia, a festival in the Attic town of Myrrhinus

December 8: Poseidea, an Athenian festival for Poseidon

December 16: a sacrifice to Zeus Horios by the Attic town of Erchia

December 19: a private sacrifice to the Wind Gods in Athens

December 26: Haloa, a festival of Demeter and Dionysus at Eleusis in Attica

December, during the second half of the month: Country Dionysia, a rural Attic festival for Dionysus

January 8: a sacrifice to Apollon Apotropaeos, Apollon Nymphegetes and the Nymphs in the Attic town of Erchia

January 9: a sacrifice to Athena in the Attic town of Erchia

January 12–15: Lenaia, an Athenian festival of Dionysus

January 27: a sacrifice to Kourotrophos, Hera, Zeus Teleios and Poseidon in Erchia

January 27: Gamelia, an Athenian celebration of the marriage of Zeus and Hera

February 2nd: a sacrifice to Dionysus in the Attic town of Erchia

February 11–13: Anthesteria, a festival for Dionysus in Athens

February 20–26: Lesser Mysteries in the town of Agrae in Attica

February 23: Diasa, an Athenian festival for Zeus Meilichios

March 6: Elaphebolia, an Athenian festival for Artemis the Huntress

March 9: Asklepieia, an Athenian festival for Asklepios

March 10–17: City Dionysia, a festival for Dionysus

March 15: private sacrifices to Kronos in Athens

March 17: Pandia, an investigation following the City Dionysia

April 4: Festival of Eros in Athens

April 6: Procession for Artemis to the Delphinion in Athens

April 16: Munichia, an Athenian festival for Artemis

April 19: Olympieia in Athens

April 20: sacrifice to Leucaspis in the Attic town of Erchia

April 21: sacrifice to the Tritopatores in the Attic town of Erchia

May 4: sacrifice to Leto, Pythian Apollon, Zeus, Hermes and the Dioskouroi in the Attic town of Erchia

May 6–7: Thargelia, an Athenian festival for Apollon

May 16: sacrifice to Zeus Epacrios in the Attic town of Erchia

May 19: Bendidia, an Athenian festival for the Thracian Goddess Bendis

May 19: sacrifice to the Menedeius in the Attic town of Erchia

May 24: Kallynteria, an Athenian rite for Athena

May 25: Plynteria, an Athenian rite for Athena

June 3: Arrephoria, an Athenian festival for Athena

June 3: sacrifice to Kourotrophos, Athena Polias, Aglauros, Zeus Polieus, Poseidon and Pandrosos in the Attic town of Erchia

June 11: sacrifice to the Tritopatores in the Attic town of Marathon

June 12: Skira, an Attic festival for Demeter

June 14: Dipolieia, an Athenian festival in honor of Zeus Polieus

June 30: Diisoteria, an Attic festival for Zeus Soter in Piraeus

June 30: sacrifice to Zeus Soter in Athens

A maenad with thyrsus

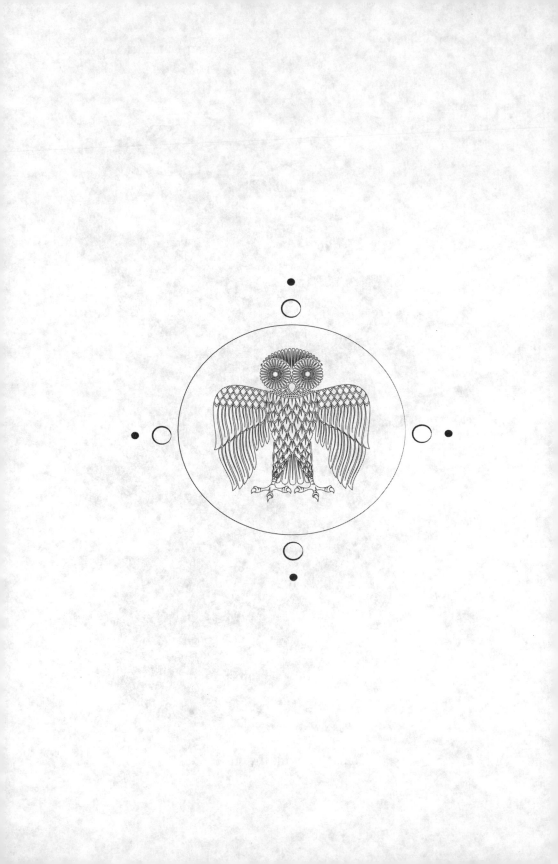

Hekatombaion
July

Once you catch a glimpse of the first sliver of the New Moon after the Summer Solstice, a new year has begun and you have entered the month of Hekatombaion. The first month is 29 days long, but also generally corresponds to the modern month of July. The name of month refers to a particular kind of sacrifice. A hecatomb is a sacrifice of a large number of animals. The name means a hundred, but it didn't always have to be that many, and could be more.

The major Athenian festival this month is the Panathenaia for Athena, with an even grander version of the festival held every fourth year. The Kronia honoring the king of the Titans was also celebrated in Attica during Hekatombaion, but was a holiday in other parts of Greece as well. The Spartan Gymnopaidia—one of the three major festivals of Sparta honoring Apollon—occurred during this month, but the exact date is unclear. You can honor Apollon at the most convenient time for you with song, dance and displays of athletic prowess.

Two days this month are set aside for the sacrifices of the Orgeones. These were members of religious societies who worshipped a particular God or hero together. On these days, the groups would make sacrifices together, to the particular hero or God each group honored. For modern Pagans, this would be a good time to make offerings with a group you regularly work with, or to reach out to other like-minded people. Take note of the following dates:

4th of the month: Aphrodisia, an Athenian festival of Aphrodite

12th of the month: Kronia, the Athenian celebration of a festival for Kronos

16th of the month: Synoikia, an Athenian holiday to celebrate the union of the towns and peoples of Attica under Athens

17th and 18th of the month: the celebrations of the Orgeones in Athens, in honor of their Gods

28th of the month: Panathenaia, a major festival of Athena in Athens

Uncertain date this month: Gymnopaidia, a Spartan festival honoring Apollon

Aphrodisia

Laughter-loving Aphrodite was born in the early days of the world. From the first chaos came Gaia the Earth and Night and Darkness. From the love of Darkness and Night came Day and the atmosphere. From Earth came the starry sky Uranus and the deep sea. From Earth and Sky came the first Gods, the Titans: graceful Tethys, golden-crowned Phoebe, Hyperion, Oceanus and all their siblings. The youngest of these was Kronos, ever scheming and lusting for power. Gaia bore more of Uranus' children, but these were no Gods. First the one-eyed Cyclopes: the Thunderer, the Lightning Flash and the Vivid One. Then three more, Kottus, Briareos and Gyges, powerful with a hundred arms and fifty heads. These children were the ones their father most despised: he tried to hide them deep in the Earth so that he would never have to see them, keeping them always in darkness. To see the suffering of her children and the contempt their father had for them angered Gaia, and she decided to punish Uranus for his cruelty. So Earth formed within herself a sickle of flint and gave it to her hundred-handed children to use against their father, but they would not. So crafty Kronos took up the blade.

He hid, and he waited. When Night came and Sky spread himself across Earth, Kronos leaped up and castrated his father. The blood fell upon Earth and from it she birthed the Furies, the giants and the nymphs. His father's genitals fell into the sea, and after a long time, they turned into the sea foam, and from the sea foam arose Aphrodite, washing gently to the shores of Cyprus. From the very beginning the Gracious Goddess ruled sweet pleasure.

On the southwestern slope of the Acropolis was a sanctuary to Aphrodite Pandemos, sensual Aphrodite of all peoples. Decorated with doves, it lay between the Propylaea—the grand main entrance to the Acropolis—and the sanctuary of the healing God Asklepios. During the Aphrodisia festival, the altar would be anointed and the sanctuary of Aphrodite Pandemos would be purified with the blood of her sacred animal, the dove. Images of the Goddess—Aphrodite Pandemos and Aphrodite Peitho, persuading Aphrodite—were carried out to be washed.

Hymn to Aphrodite

Shimmering-throned immortal Aphrodite,
Daughter of Zeus, Enchantress, I implore thee,
Spare me, O queen, this agony and anguish,
Crush not my spirit

Whenever before thou has hearkened to me—
To my voice calling to thee in the distance,
And heeding, thou hast come, leaving
thy father's
Golden dominions,

With chariot yoked to thy fleet-winged coursers,
Fluttering swift pinions over earth's darkness,
And bringing thee through the infinite, gliding
Downwards from heaven,

Then, soon they arrived and thou,
blessed goddess,
With divine countenance smiling, didst ask me
What new woe had befallen me now and why,
Thus I had called thee.

What in my mad heart was my greatest desire,
Who was it now that must feel my allurements,
Who was the fair one that must be persuaded,
Who wronged thee Sappho?

For if now she flees, quickly she shall follow
And if she spurns gifts, soon shall she offer them
Yea, if she knows not love, soon shall she feel it
Even reluctant.

Come then, I pray, grant me surcease
from sorrow,
Drive away care, I beseech thee, O goddess
Fulfill for me what I yearn to accomplish,
Be thou my ally.

Sappho Poem 1, (6th century BCE)
−tr . Edwin Marion Cox, 1925

Kronia

The reign of Kronos over Earth and Heaven was the golden age, a time when humankind lived together in peace, sharing the unlimited abundance of land and sea. Free from toil and violence, they did not know the ship, the sword or the plow—the world simply provided. When his son Zeus overthrew Kronos, the golden age came to an end. Silver followed gold, then bronze and finally iron. Violence, suffering and work increased with each turn.

In one version of the story, Kronos remains—perhaps even now—on a faraway island, sleeping through these fallen ages of the world. In another, Zeus punishes his father with captivity in the Underworld. Even in his confinement, Kronos rules the Isle of the Blessed and lucky are those few mortal souls who come under his reign.

Zeus maintains order in the universe through structure and social restraint. Not so with Kronos, and his festival had a carnivalesque tone. In the festival of Kronia, slaves dined with their masters, a social inversion that briefly echoed the egalitarian ease of the golden age. Kronia occurs at the end of the grain harvest, a time that naturally recalls the peace that plenty can bring.

From the Orphic Hymn to Kronos (Saturn)

Ethereal father, mighty Titan, hear,
Great fire of Gods and men, whom all revere,
Endued with various council, pure and strong,
To whom perfection and decrease belong.
Consumed by thee all forms that hourly die,
By thee restored, their former place supply.
The world immense in everlasting chains,

Strong and ineffable thy power contains
Father of vast eternity, divine,
O mighty Saturn, various speech is thine.
Blossom of earth and of the starry skies,
Husband of Rhea, and Prometheus wife.
Obstetric Nature, venerable root,
From which the various forms of being shoot,
No parts peculiar can thy power enclose,
Diffused through all, from which the world arose.
O, best of beings, of a subtle mind,
Propitious hear to holy prayers inclined.
The sacred rites benevolent attend,
And grant a blameless life, a blessed end.

−tr. Thomas Taylor, 1792, spelling modernized
by M. Borden

Rhea presents a swaddled stone to Cronus.

Panathenaia

When she sprang screaming from the head of Zeus onto the shores of Triton, the owl-eyed maiden Athena was already clad in armor, already shaking her spear, her battle cry already ringing through the world. The sea roared back and the mountains rumbled in fear. Helios himself was frozen in the sky, staring until she lowered her weapons and removed her armor.

The Virgin Goddess competed with Poseidon for the patronage of Athens, where snake-tailed Cecrops was king. The Earthshaker created horses and struck his trident into the ground, making a salt spring come bubbling forth. Wise Athena gave the olive tree, and the king judged in her favor. And so the Earthborn Cecrops set up her statue and was the first to offer sacrifices to the Industrious Goddess, to the One Who Fights on the Front Line of Battle. He had also instituted worship of Zeus, but allowed only cakes to be offered to the immortal Gods and not living animals.

Lovely Athena Parthenos would take no man or God as her husband, but Hephaistos desired her and from his lust the child Erechtheus was born from the stone of the Acropolis. Athena took the baby, put him in a closed basket and gave it to the three daughters of King Cecrops—Herse, Aglauros and Pandrosos—to guard, telling them not to look inside it. Defying the will of the Goddess, two of the girls lifted the lid of the basket and saw a serpent lurking within it. They were driven mad by the sight and threw themselves off of the Acropolis, to their deaths. The Goddess raised the baby Erechtheus herself. He became king of Athens after Cecrops and had a shrine on the Acropolis.

The city of Athens celebrated Athena's birthday each year with the Panathenaia and held an especially grand version every four years. The largest celebration in Athens, the Panathenaia was a city-wide, multi-day festival in honor of Athena. For nine months beforehand, specially chosen women of the city had been weaving a peplos—a dress—for the Goddess. It was brightly colored with yellow and blue and on the middle stripe of it, they worked scenes of the battle between the Gods and the giants. It was originally a human-sized dress, made to fit the life-sized archaic statue. Once the statue was a wondrous work of gold and ivory over 30 feet tall, the peplos was as large as a sail. Presenting the peplos to the statue of the Goddess was the central event of the celebration, and it was carried in a grand procession through the city, along with musicians, athletes, sacrificial animals, priests, officials and people.

The festivities begin the evening before the procession with an all-night party at the Acropolis at which the young people of the city sing a paean—a song of praise—for Athena and sing and dance in honor of the Goddess. In the morning, runners light torches from the fire on the altar of Eros about two miles away—near the old altar of Prometheus in the Academy, the grove made famous by Socrates. Whoever first brings a still-lit torch to the altar of Athena on the Acropolis receives a water jug as the first prize of the festival.

The great procession forms near the Dipylon Gate, where the road to Eleusis enters the city. At the front are the ergastinai—a pair of women representing all those who wove and worked the peplos. Following them are young women carrying bowls, jugs, jars and an incense burner, all for the sacrifice. There are 100 girls in gold jewelry and necklaces of figs, the kanephoroi who carry the barley baskets on their heads. In one basket is hidden the sacrificial knife. The peplos itself is attached to a ship set on wheels and is sailed through the streets.

The women and girls are followed by the thallotrophoi, the old men carrying olive branches who have been chosen for their good looks. Freed slaves and foreigners join in at the end, carrying oak branches. There are young men in purple robes carrying trays of cakes and honeycombs. There are athletes on foot and on horseback. Then come the chariots, some with two horses and some with four, carrying the older men in their hoplite armor.

Within all are the victims, at least 100 white cows, and sometimes many more. There are sheep and goats as well, and at least one cow and a suit of armor for each city or town owing tribute to Athens, as many as 400. They are driven forward through the streets, their steps accompanied by music, because the lyre and the pipe attend every sacrifice.

The procession follows the Panathenaic Way, winding through the working-class Kerameikos through the Agora and to the foot of the Acropolis. They ascend to the altar of Athena, high on the rock with the temple behind and a girl gives the kanoun—the barley basket—to the priests, passing the knife within as well. The Goddess is presented with the gleaming peplos and the people take handfuls of grain to throw at the animals to purify the offering. The animals' throats are cut at the altar and thousands of voices raise the cry in the air. One animal is offered in front of Athena Nike, and the old law was that for each cow given to Athena, a sheep was offered to Pandrosos, the daughter of Cecrops, the first Athenian king. After the Gods' portions, the meat is cooked and given to the participants and then taken down to the Kerameikos and distributed in the city.

Over the next two days are many competitions. Among the greatest honors are the rhapsodes, the competitive poetry recitations and musical and dramatic competitions that draw the best poets, playwrights and musicians from all over Greece. The prizes are good, but it is a great honor to win a contest at the Panathenaia. Then come the agones, the athletic competitions. There are honors for the victors and riches as well: gilded wreaths, money and jugs of oil pressed from the grove Athena herself planted. The amphorae were specially decorated with black-figure images of Athena brandishing her spear and depictions of the particular athletic event. These events include horse races, foot races, races that begin on chariot and end on foot, the pentathlon, wrestling, boxing, javelin throwing from horseback and a contest of ships. There is a Pyrrhic dance performed in armor for Athena to celebrate defeat of the Titans, and a contest of evandria—manly excellence—that includes size, strength, and demonstrations of prowess.

Excerpt from Homeric Hymn 11

Of Pallas Athena, guardian of the city, I begin to
sing. Dread is she, and with Ares she loves deeds
of war, the sack of cities and the shouting and
the battle. It is she who saves the people as they
go out to war and come back.

Hail, goddess, and give us good fortune
with happiness!

−tr. Hugh Evelyn-White, 1914

Gymnopaidia

The Festival of Naked Youths, the Gymnopaidia was an annual, late summer festival in Sparta. Anyone engaging in athletic practice and competition was habitually naked in ancient Greece. Honoring Apollon, the Gymnopaidia centered around choral performances and ritual combat. Choirs of naked men competed, enduring long days in the unforgiving heat. The leader of each chorus group wore a crown of feathers or leaves arranged to look like feathers to honor the fallen dead of historic battles.

The festival took place over several days. The evening before the first day of festivities, there participants gathered for a night sacrifice of a puppy to Enyalios—a son or epithet of Ares. Over subsequent days, boys and men competed in dancing, singing and displays of athleticism. The air was thick with hymns to Spartan Gods and heroes.

The ritual fight of the epheboi—boys old enough to begin training for war—was a central element of the Gymnopaidia. They did not use weapons, proving themselves by engaging with teeth and fists, wrestling with arms and feet. This fight took place on a small island in a marsh, and the winners pushed the losers into the water. Older men who had remained unmarried were not allowed to take part in the festivities, but they were otherwise open to both Spartans and foreign visitors.

Excerpt from Hymn to Apollon by Callimachus

Apollo will honour the choir, since it sings
according to his heart; for Apollo hath power, for
that he sitteth on the right hand of Zeus. Nor will
the choir sing of Phoebus for one day only. He is
a copious theme of song; who would not readily
sing of Phoebus?

—tr. A.W. Mair, 1921

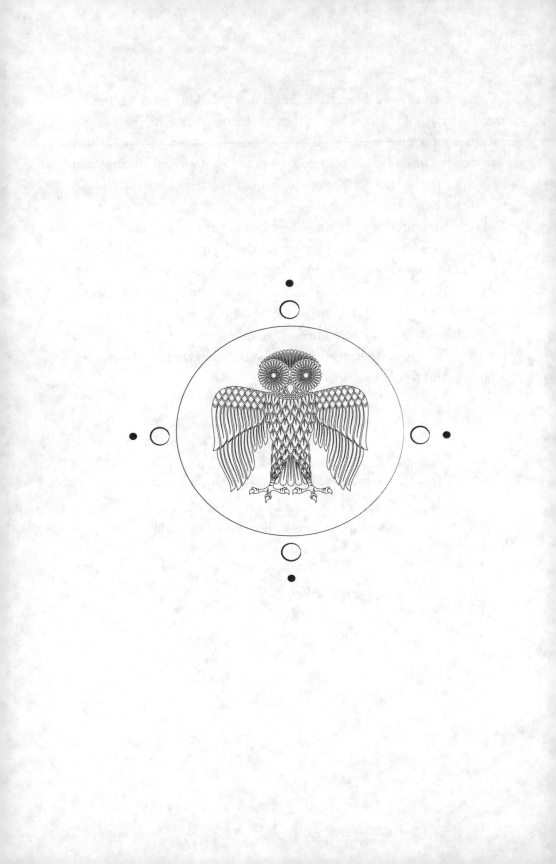

Metageitnion
August

In Metageitnion, the grass has dried up, the mountainsides are brown and everything is dusty. The major festival this month is Karneia, one of the three prominent Spartan festivals for Apollon. The Karneia particularly celebrates military life. Athens also celebrates Apollon in a minor festival, the Metageitnia, which gives the month its name. Also in Athens is the Eleusinia, another smaller festival that is not the same as the Eleusinian Mysteries a few weeks later in the month of Boedromion. The Eleusinia was held the second and fourth years of each Olympiad (a four-year period.) The festival on second years was minor and on fourth years was greater. It consisted of a procession, sacrifices and athletic contests with grain as the prize.

There are several sacrifices that happen this month from the town of Erchia in Attica. Little is known about these offerings beyond the epithets of the Gods used in the sacrifice. The first of these is offered to Kourotropos, Hekate and Artemis. "Kourotrophos" means "the one who brings up boys" and is an epithet of many Goddesses, including Artemis. Hekate and Artemis are well known as night-roaming companions, and are both also associated with midwifery, perhaps linking them to the Kourotrophos epithet. The next is a sacrifice to unspecified heroines. There are two of these in the year, and no specific names are known. This would be a good day to honor any heroines of your own, Greek or otherwise. The third sacrifice is offered to Hera Telchinia, Hera of the Telchines. These mythical creatures of the Dodecanese islands in the eastern Aegean had the heads of dogs and flippers in place of hands. They had sorcerous powers and worshipped Hera in several cities on the island of Rhodes. The last of the Erchian sacrifices this month is to Zeus Epoptes, Zeus the Overseer. Take note of the following dates:

7th–15th of the month: Karneia, a Spartan festival in honor of Apollon

15th –18th of the month: Eleusinia, an Athenian festival distinct from the Eleusinian mysteries

16th of the month: a sacrifice to Kourotrophos, Hekate and Artemis from Erchia

19th of the month: a sacrifice to the Heroines from Erchia

20th of the month: a sacrifice to Hera Telchinia from the town of Erchia

25th of the month: a sacrifice to Zeus Epoptes from Erchia

Uncertain date this month: Metageitnia, an Attic festival for Apollon

Uncertain date this month: a festival for Herakles in the Attic town Kynosarges

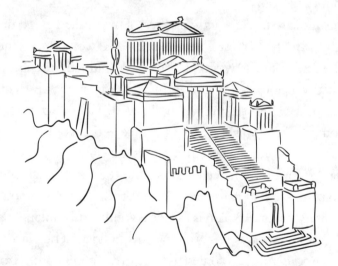

Karneia

Karneia, the most important festival of the Spartans occurred during the month of Karneios, which corresponded to the Athenian month of Metageitnion. During the festival in honor of Apollon Karneios—protector of the flocks—Sparta would not engage in warfare. The Spartans took this so seriously that they delayed going to assist Athens against the Persians at the battle of Marathon, and by the time they arrived, the Athenians had defeated the armies of Darius the Great without their help.

One of the festival events was a race of boys called graperunners (even though the grape harvest is still far off.) One would be clothed in wool and the rest naked as was typical in Greek athletic events. The boy in wool began before the others, and if the rest caught up to him or overtook him, it was a blessing for the harvest. Failing to catch him was a poor omen. There was also a ram sacrifice—the wool-clad runner represented the ram, and the ram then represents him.

The Spartans were fiercely warlike and the festival included ritual acts symbolizing the life of a soldier, such as feasts in tents as you would see in a military camp. Apollon is the ideal youth, and dancing by the young people of the city was important at this holiday. The Karneia also had a very famous musical contest which drew competitors from all over Greece. As soon as Apollon was born, he called for a lyre to be brought to him and he invented the paean, a hymn of thanksgiving.

Excerpts from Hymn to Apollon by Callimachus

How the laurel branch of Apollo trembles! How trembles all the shrine! Away, away, he that is sinful! The Delian palm nods pleasantly of a sudden and the swan in the air sings sweetly. The god is no longer far away. And ye, young men, prepare ye for song and for the dance.

Not unto everyone doth Apollo appear, but unto him that is good. Whoso hath seen Apollo, he is great—whoso hath not seen him, he is of low estate. We shall see thee, O Archer, and we shall never be lowly.

Golden is the tunic of Apollo and golden his mantle, his lyre and his Lyctian bow and his quiver: golden too are his sandals, for rich in gold is Apollo, rich also in possessions, by Pytho mightst thou guess. And ever beautiful is he and ever young.

None is so abundant in skill as Apollo. To him belongs the archer, to him the minstrel—for unto Apollo is given in keeping alike archery and song. His are the lots of the diviner and his the seers and from Phoebus do leeches know the deferring of death.

O Apollo! Many there be that call thee Boëdromius, and many there be that call thee Clarius: everywhere is thy name on the lips of many. But I call thee Carneius for such is the manner of my fathers. Sparta, O Carneius! Hië, Hië, Carneius! Lord of many prayers, thine altars wear flowers in spring, even all the pied flowers which the Hours lead forth when Zephyrus breathes dew, and in winter the sweet crocus. Undying evermore is thy fire, nor ever doth the ash feed about the coals of yester-even. Greatly, indeed, did Phoebus rejoice as the belted warriors of Enyo danced with the yellow-haired Libyan women, when the appointed season of the Carnean feast came round. No other dance more divine hath Apollo beheld.

Hië, Hië, Paeëon, we hear—since this refrain did the Delphian folk first invent, what time thou didst display the archery of thy golden bow. As thou wert going down to Pytho, there met thee a beast unearthly, a dread snake. And him thou didst slay, shooting swift arrows one upon the other; and the folk cried "Hië, Hië, Paeëon, shoot an arrow!" A helper from the first thy mother bare thee, and ever since that is thy praise.

—tr. A.W. Mair, 1921

Metageitnia

Leto was the daughter of Titans Coeus (intelligence) and Phoebe (radiance). She caught the ever-wandering eye of Zeus and became pregnant with his twin children. She began looking for a place to give birth, but every city and town refused to welcome her in, fearing the retribution of Hera, the Queen of Heaven. Given no welcome, weary Leto wandered over the world, coming at last to Delos, the drifting, shifting island. It only finally became still and rooted with the birth of Apollon. There she labored for nine days, grasping a palm tree and an olive tree to steady herself through the pains. She birthed Artemis first, who immediately took up her duties as a Goddess of midwives and childbirth and assisted her mother as the very next day she gave birth to far-shooting Apollon. The twins were bright—the sunlight and the moonlight. Talented with the bow, both mighty hunters and athletes, Artemis rules the wild lands and the mountaintops, Apollon music, poetry and the healing arts. Hers are all the untamed places, his the civilized world. They remained intensely faithful to their mother, on one occasion shooting down the fourteen children of Niobe, a woman who foolishly boasted that she was better than Leto because she had so many more children. There are no fiercer protectors than the divine twins.

Very little is known about the lesser festival of Metageitnia. It celebrates Apollon Agyieus, Apollon of the Street. He was worshipped under this epithet as a protector of the entrances of houses, and he was represented by an obelisk or other upright, pointed stone near the door of a home. These stones were often decorated with small offerings—ribbons and garlands of plants sacred to Apollon, such as bay or myrtle. He can drive away all darkness, and this day would be a good time to ask for his protection on your home.

Heraklea

Worshipped sometimes as a hero and sometimes as a God, Herakles was the son of Zeus and the mortal woman Alcmene. His name means "the glory of Hera," and indeed, his works brought great renown. Hera despised him and tormented him with fits of madness. During one of these, not knowing himself, the hero killed his own children. He fled to Delphi, begging the oracle of Apollon to guide him in purifying himself of the horrible crime. The oracle—likely influenced by Hera—told him to enter into the service of the cruel king Eurystheus, who set him fourteen impossible tasks. These were his famed twelve labors, because his taskmaster refused to accept two of them. He overcame these and went on to have many other adventures. Eventually he was killed by trickery and poison from his own arrows. Resisting to the very end, he built his own funeral pyre even as the poison was leeching

Heracles wrestling the Nemean Lion

his great strength. His friend Philoctetes lit it after he died, and Herakles' mortal body burned away while his immortal spirit rose to Olympus. There he wed Hebe, a Goddess of Youth.

This date is associated with a festival of Herakles in a gymnasium in the town of Kynosarges near Athens. The ancient Greeks tended toward xenophobia, but this festival was known for allowing non-citizens and children of foreign-born parents to participate in its activities, which was not typical. The cult of Herakles allowed priests with foreign-born parents as well. Generally speaking, Herakles was a hero of the people—he enjoyed drink and banquets, and his festivals had feasts as a central part of the celebrations, with members of the lower classes chosen to be special companions for Herakles while he dined.

In addition to banquets, ways to honor Herakles include overcoming unjust treatment, feats of strength and displays of vigor.

Homeric Hymn 15, to Heracles the Lion-Hearted

I will sing of Heracles, the son of Zeus and much the mightiest of men on earth. Alcmena bare him in Thebes, the city of lovely dances, when the dark-clouded Son of Cronos had lain with her. Once he used to wander over unmeasured tracts of land and sea at the bidding of King Eurystheus, and himself did many deeds of violence and endured many; but now he lives happily in the glorious home of snowy Olympus, and has neat-ankled Hebe for his wife.

Hail, lord, son of Zeus. Give me success and prosperity.

—tr. Hugh Evelyn-White, 1914

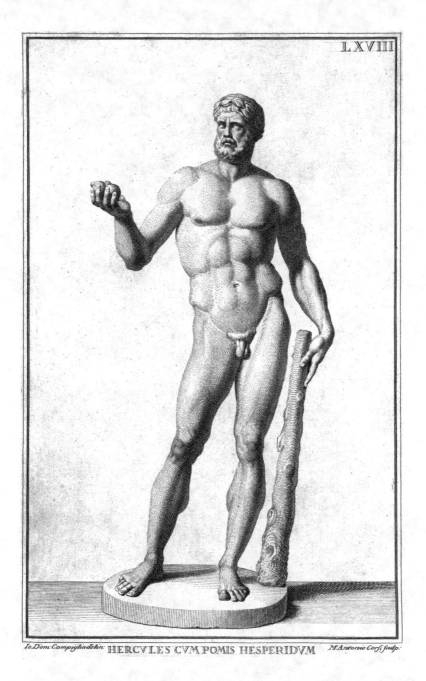

LXVIII

Io. Dom. Campigliadelin. HERCVLES CVM POMIS HESPERIDVM M. Antonio Corsi sculp.

Boedromion
September

As the military campaigning season comes to an end, the city honors its dead in the Genesia. On the 12th, Athenians celebrate the establishment of their democracy. The major festival in Boedromion is the Eleusinian Mysteries, which begin for initiates on the 15th, with preparatory rites beginning on the 13th. The entire festival lasted at least six days from the 15th and could be longer.

There are three sacrifices recorded outside Athens this month. The first is a sacrifice to Basile, an Attic heroine, in Erchia. She was given a female white lamb, which was offered in its entirety and not consumed by the people. This is typical of hero worship—the Gods' sacrifices are burned on a raised altar and are shared so that the people dine with the Gods. Hero worship is a form of chthonic worship, in which offerings are poured into a pit (because the dead are in the ground.) These are not shared by the living.

Later in the month the Attic town of Teithras offered a sacrifice to Athena and Erchia offered to the nymphs, Achelous, Alochus, Hermes and Gaia on the same day. A son of the Titans Tethys and Oceanus, Achelous is a river God mentioned in the Iliad for his strength. He famously fought against Herakles in the form of a bull in an unsuccessful attempt to win the hand of Deianeira. His horn was torn off in the process and the water spirits turned it into a cornucopia. He went on to father nymphs, also named in this sacrifice. Alochus simply means "wife" but the identity of the wife of Achelous is unclear. The river Achelous itself is not in Attica or near Erchia. Called King Achelous by Homer, he was worshipped throughout the Greek world as the greatest of rivers. If you wish to celebrate on this day, offer to your local river Gods and include Achelous as well. Take note of the following dates:

4th of the month: a sacrifice to Basile by the Attic town of Erchia

5th of the month: Genesia, an Athenian feast of the dead

6th of the month: Charisteria, an Athenian sacrifice of thanksgiving to Artemis Agrotera

12th of the month: Democratia in Athens

15th–20th of the month: Eleusinian Mysteries in Attica

18th of the month: Epidauria, an Attic festival for Asclepius on the 4th day of the Mysteries

25th of the month: Boedromia, an Athenian feast of thanksgiving to Apollon

27th of the month: a sacrifice to Athena by the Attic town of Teithras

27th of the month: a sacrifice to the nymphs, Achelous, Alochus, Hermes and Gaia by Erchia

Genesia

The Genesia festival was a state celebration honoring the dead. It may have originally been a family festival in which people honored their personal dead, but this also happened throughout the year.

The ancient Greeks generally had a dim view of the afterlife. When a person died, the soul left the body and was escorted to the Underworld by Hekate or Hermes. Once the funeral was finished, the soul crossed the rivers, never to return. Ghosts could advocate with the living for their burial rituals to be completed, but otherwise, once they had entered the kingdom of Hades, souls lost their sense of identity and drifted about as mere shadows of their former selves. A few entered the blissful fields of Elisium and a few endured just punishment, but for most people the only way to cheat death was through fame—to live on through remembrance by the living. The dead resided in a world far from the living and at the same time the dead inhabited their graves and could be contacted there.

Tending the graves of ancestors was an important obligation. Corpses—particularly of the untimely dead—were also a potent source of magic. Ghost stories were common in ancient Greece, and the spirits of the dead could appear as snakes. Because the dead live in the Earth—not just abstractly, but in the actual dirt at their gravesites—offerings to them were poured into the ground. They were capable of exchange with the living in a similar way to Gods: they received offerings and were able to give blessings in return. While not especially powerful, they could also send curses and bad luck, and it was important to appease them. Regular offerings were a sure way to assuage their anger and keep their favor, and a way to summon them, because necromancy was occasionally practiced.

Offerings—particularly blood offerings—enabled the shades of the dead to become conscious, recall themselves and converse with the living.

The offerings are the same, but the act of venerating the dead and the Gods of the dead is an inversion of Olympian worship. Libations and sacrifices are poured into a pit, to go downwards rather than being burnt so the smoke rises from the raised Olympian altar. Sacrifices and libations for the dead are done at night and the best animals for the purpose are black. Worshipping the Gods is best done with clean hands and garlanded hair whereas contact with the dead requires purification afterwards.

Heroes received this chthonic worship as well as the personal dead. Some of the Underworld powers are terrible, but a few are kindly, particularly those associated with the home and ancestors. This form of worship is not inherently evil—like all the other propitiation of the Greeks, it is amoral and used to accomplish many ends.

Odyssey, Book 11, lines 24-38

I drew my sword and dug the trench a cubit each way. I made a drink-offering to all the dead, first with honey and milk, then with wine, and thirdly with water, and I sprinkled white barley meal over the whole, praying earnestly to the poor feckless ghosts, and promising them that when I got back to Ithaca I would sacrifice a barren heifer for them, the best I had, and would load the pyre with good things. I also particularly promised that Teiresias should have a black sheep to himself, the best in all my flocks. When I had prayed sufficiently to the dead, I cut the throats of the two sheep and let the blood run into the trench, whereon the ghosts came trooping up from Erebus.

-tr. Samuel Butler, 1900

Charisteria for Artemis Agrotera

When the young Goddess Artemis left Delos, the island of her birth, she came to Attica and there she learned to hunt. To honor Artemis Agrotera—Artemis the Huntress—the Athenians built a temple to her outside the walls of Athens. There she was worshipped alongside Enyalios, a name of Ares. The war God had very little cult of his own, and this is one of few sites where he was venerated and received sacrifice.

This temple became the site of a votive offering so massive that it had to be spread over many years. The basic relationship between humans and Gods in Greece is one of exchange—a gift for a gift. In times of need, a person or a state could ask a God for help and vow a specific sacrifice in return once the help was delivered. When the situation was adequately resolved, this sort of vow was not one to be broken, and votive offerings of many kinds are some of the most common objects found in temples. These can be objects as well as sacrifices, for example, a soldier aided in battle might give some of his armor as a votive offering.

The Spartans had a regular practice of sacrificing a goat to Artemis Agrotera before joining in battle, and animals were sacrificed to many Gods on the battlefield. During the Persian War, the Athenians were vastly outnumbered by the Persians at the battle of Marathon in 490 BCE. They numbered ten or eleven thousand, while Darius the Great fielded many times that number. Before leaving for the battle, the Athenian government vowed to Artemis Agrotera a sacrifice of one female goat for every Persian soldier they were able to kill. The Athenians made their battleline weak in the middle, so that the Persian forces would break through and then find themselves surrounded.

This strategy was so effective that the final death toll was 192 fallen Greeks and 6,400 Persians.

This was a great victory and a small problem—Athens didn't have nearly enough goats! To fulfill their vow, the Athenians sacrificed 500 female goats each year for well over a century. They did this on the 6th of Boedromion, which was already a festival of Artemis, as the 6th of every month celebrates her birthday. It is close to the anniversary of Marathon, but probably not the exact date. Over time, the sacrifice came to be a remembrance of the battle itself. The festival was organized by the chief military officer in the state and featured a parade of soldiers in training marching to the temple in addition to the sacrifice.

When people offer sacrifice freely to the Gods as a way of gaining their favor, the Gods may accept the sacrifice without being obliged to help the person offering. While a vow, on the other hand, may be accompanied by an initial offering, the main sacrifice is received by the Gods after help has been given as a way to ensure the exchange. A votive offering is an expression of gratitude, of thanksgiving or *charisteria*—which gives this holiday its name.

Artemis the Huntress

Eleusinian Mysteries

By offering assurance of the eternal care of the Gods in the lives and afterlives of initiates, the Mysteries of Eleusis stand in stark contrast to the generally dim view ancient Greeka had of death. They are also distinct from most other Greek religious practices because of their deeply personal nature. Most Greek festivals were civic in character and supported the relationship between a state and the Gods that protected it and ensured its prosperity. The mysteries at Eleusis offered a spiritual experience that would have been less available at public sacrifices.

These rites are first and foremost secrets—they could not be written about or spoken of, even with fellow initiates. To do so was a crime in Athens and people were prosecuted for it. For this reason, there is little information available about the main ritual actions and what does exist comes from Christian criticism, as the early church—a mystery cult itself at the time—viewed the rites of Eleusis as their competition. This is largely because of their spiritual character. Most modern people take for granted the spiritual nature of religion, but that understanding is deeply influenced by Christianity, which at its inception was a mystery cult. Initiates of the Eleusinian Mysteries anticipated a happy afterlife—they had faced the inevitability of death and were promised the comfort of the Goddess afterwards. In the Homeric Hymns, the Mysteries of Eleusis were taught by Demeter herself.

THE HYMN

Lovely Persephone was playing in a meadow, away from her mother. Picking flowers, she came upon a magnificent narcissus with the sweetest perfume. Captivated by its beauty, the girl reached to pick the flower which was formed for this very purpose—Earth herself was in on the plan. In that moment, a gaping crack split the soft-blossomed field, and the Lord of Many Names rushed up in his golden chariot, and snatched Persephone away, just as merciless death seizes all. She screamed and shrieked and begged her father Zeus for help, not knowing that the whole thing was arranged at his command. The place was remote and her cries were heard only by kind-hearted Hekate of the gleaming hair and Helios, the radiant son of Hyperion. She kept hope as long as she could see the sunlight playing over land, sky and sea and finally her cries echoed over the mountains, through the deep waters and came to the ears of her immortal mother.

Hearing her daughter's anguish, Demeter tore her veil and rushed out to find her. She looked in all the land and all the sea but no one told her where Persephone had gone or what her cry might mean. For nine days without even a pause to bathe, the Goddess wandered the Earth with torches, depriving herself of nectar and ambrosia, the sweet sustenance of the immortal Gods. As the sunlight gleamed over the tenth morning, torch-bearing Hekate came to Demeter and told her that she, too, had heard the girl's cries. Together they rushed to Helios, knowing that the Sun sees all things that happen upon Earth. Helios told Demeter the truth and that Zeus lay behind it all. Trying to soothe her heart, he reminded her that Hades was also immortal, a mighty son of Kronos and a worthy husband for her daughter. Demeter was not consoled and a dread rage burned in her heart for her brother Zeus, Persephone's father.

Avoiding Olympus, Zeus and the Gods, Demeter disguised her divine beauty and kept to the human world. No one suspected until she came to Eleusis. She sat broken hearted under an olive tree by the well, watching the people come draw their water, but appeared to their eyes as an old woman, the sort who might raise up the children of others. The king of Eleusis at that time was Celeus and his four daughters came with bronze pitchers to carry their water. They saw the old woman, asked why she hadn't come into the town and assured her that she would be welcomed. She gave them a false name and told a tale of being captured by pirates and escaping to wander through the region until she came there. The lovely daughters of Celeus with hair like crocuses had a young brother so they ran back up to town and got permission from their mother to hire the old woman as a nurse to help raise him. Dark robed and veiled, Demeter followed them to where their mother Metaneira waited with her infant son Triptolemus in the courtyard of their house. As she stood on the threshold, the Goddess showed her divinity, glowing with light and growing tall enough to fill the doorway of that proud house. Metaneira jumped up to give her couch to the divine guest, but Demeter waited until a servant brought a chair. Her hosts brought her food and drink but she refused, too full of longing for her child to refresh herself. She kept her eyes down as she sat in silence, the grief that filled her heart apparent to all. Finally the servant Iambe began to ply the immortal Goddess with jokes, appealing to the coarsest humor to cheer Demeter's heart. Once their guest smiled and laughed, Metaneira offered her sweet wine, but the daughter of Kronos asked instead for her host to mix barley meal and water with mint.

Metaneira offered the Goddess a position in the household and Demeter agreed to raise up the young prince. He was richly blessed and seemed like a God to all who gazed on him, for his immortal nurse anointed him with ambrosia and hid him at night in fire. This would have made him immortal, but when his mother saw what was happening, fearing for her child, she spoke ill of the nurse. Anger burned again in Demeter's heart and she snatched the boy out of the blaze and swore an oath on the Styx that the child would never escape death and the Fates, but that he would be blessed from being in her care. She also cursed that Eleusis would always know war. At last Demeter told her name to Metaneira—who had only seen that she was a Goddess but

Demeter, the Queen of the Harvest Festivals.

not guessed her identity—and demanded that a temple and an altar be raised for her on the hill above the well where she had first met the daughters of Celeus. Last, she promised to teach sacred rituals that would appease her heart if the people of Eleusis would carry them out faithfully. As she spoke, Demeter let fall the appearance of old age and showed her immortal beauty, which drifted out like a perfume from her radiant garments. The Goddess shone so brightly that the house flashed like it had been struck by lightning and then she disappeared.

Metaneira fell to knees, unable to utter a word from her awe-filled heart. Her daughters took over the care of the prince, but the baby was not pleased with the change and his heart longed for the gentle love of his divine nurse. Celeus ordered the people of the town to build the temple as Demeter had instructed, and so the boy thrived as he grew.

Demeter remained in her new temple and continued to stay away from the councils of the immortal Gods on Olympus and undistracted by the tasks of caring for the boy, her heart turned again to her grief and anger. These were felt by all on Earth. The oxen pulled the plough and the people threw barley in the furrows but Demeter kept every seed covered in dirt, not allowing so much as a single shoot to break through to the Sun. Pitiless famine spread everywhere and even threatened the sacrifices to the Gods. Finally Zeus sent Iris the messenger to summon Demeter to Olympus, but Demeter would not go. He sent another God and another until all the immortals had begged her with gifts and peace offerings, but dark-robed Demeter refused. She would neither attend Zeus in Olympus nor allow a single seed to sprout until she saw Persephone with her own eyes.

Then Zeus sent Hermes to dark-haired Hades in the depths of Erebus, where he sat with his reluctant bride. The caduceus-bearing slayer of Argus explained Demeter's wrath to the Lord of the Dead and Hades immediately told wise Persephone to go to her mother. He assured her that he would be a worthy husband and that when she ruled in the Underworld, she would rule over all living creatures. "Those who do you any wrong," he told her, "and do not honor your rites and propriate you with sacrifices will be met with reckoning." And the Host of Multitudes gave her a bit of pomegranate to eat to ensure that she would return to his house. Persephone leapt up joyfully and joined Hermes in her husband's golden chariot.

They drove straight to Eleusis and when Demeter of the splendid crown saw her daughter, she rushed out of her temple. Persephone jumped down from the chariot and threw her arms around her mother's neck. Holding her child joyfully in her arms, Demeter sensed that she had been deceived by some trick. She knew that if her daughter had eaten anything in the Underworld, then she must spend a third of her year there. Persephone related the whole tale of her abduction and told her mother that she had eaten the pomegranate seeds. The Two Ladies spent the whole day in their joyful reunion and Hekate joined them and from that time on she attended Royal Persephone.

Cloud-gathering Zeus sent Rhea to them. The mighty Goddesses were standing in a dry and barren plain because Demeter still kept all the seeds hidden in the soil. When Rhea brought them the word of Zeus the Loud Thunderer that he would allow Persephone to spend two-thirds of her year on Earth in the light of the Sun, then the first shoots of Spring rose up and soon the stalks tilted over, heavy with grain. The broad plain filled with flowers and green leaves and Demeter went to the kings and nobles of Eleusis and taught them her mysteries and showed them how to perform her sacred rites. These mysteries are kept secret and never violated because the awe of the Gods silences the voice.

The Goddess of Goddesses enacted all this and then went up to Olympus with Persephone, where they joined mighty Zeus. Blessed is the mortal loved by these Gods for they send the Giver of Wealth as a guest to that house.

THE TEMPLE

These mysteries, a gift of Demeter to humankind, were set down in Eleusis where the Athenians believed that grain was first sown. They were gifted to all—old and young, men and women, slaves and free—so long as they could speak Greek. The shrine at Eleusis is from at least the Mycenaean period and the Mysteries endured for a thousand years. The priesthood who oversaw the rites were drawn from two ancient clans, the Kerykes and the Eumolpidai, descended from the kings who welcomed Demeter to Eleusis in her grief and first tended her temple. These clans also provided the mystagogoi who acted as individual guides to the ceremonies, preventing new initiates from violating any custom.

The temple itself was called the Telesterion, the Hall of Initiation. Unlike most temples, it was used for congregational worship and at its largest it could hold ten thousand. Its columns were said to be like a forest. In the very center was the Anaktoron—a central shrine or small temple within the temple. The Sacred Items were kept in the Anaktoron the rest of the year, and only brought out for the Mysteries. The name means "House of the King," from the Mycenaean word *anax* (king.) Only the hierophant—the one priest from the clan of Eumolpos who revealed the Sacred Items—could enter there.

PREPARATIONS

Before the Mysteries were to begin, messengers were sent to all cities asking them to declare a 55-day truce so that pilgrims to Eleusis from all regions would not need to be concerned for their safety. On the 13th of Boedromion young soldiers in training went to Eleusis and on the 14th escorted the *hiera*—Holy Things or Sacred Items—from Eleusis to Athens—to the Eleusinion at the foot of the Acropolis. The Sacred Items were carried in *kistai*—

Triptolemos Demi-God of the
Eleusinian Mysteries

round boxes tied with purple ribbons. Priestesses carried these in a
wagon but had to stop at river crossings to carry them over by hand.

THE RITES

Day One—The Gathering. On the 15th the *mystai* (soon-to-be-ini-
tiates) gather in the Painted Portico in the Agora in Athens to declare
themselves before the priests of the festival and pay their fees of fifteen
drachmas, which was about ten days' wages. They should be free of
any blood guilt and be spiritually fit by living justly and having no evil
intentions. Seven months prior in the month of Anthesterion, mystai
were supposed to have been initiated into the lesser mysteries in the
town of Agrai before becoming initiates at Eleusis. They were also

expected to fast from fish, fowl, beans, apples, pomegranates and eggs as these specific foods were forbidden throughout the mysteries. The day of Gathering was especially auspicious when it fell on a Full Moon.

Day Two—Seaward Initiates. On the 16th the mystai undergo purification rites to keep from approaching the sanctuary in an impure state. These consist of sea bathing for purification and being sprinkled with pigs' blood for atonement. They are carried to the sea in carts and then each mystes carries a piglet into the water and immerses both themselves and the pig beneath the waves. They return to Athens to sacrifice the pigs. Sharks could be attracted if this were attempted in the sea and shark attack is a very ill omen. The mystai are sprinkled with the sacrificial blood to atone for any guilt and remove any miasma that might be lingering on them.

Day Three—Hither the Victims. On the 17th there were state sacrifices to the Two Goddesses. They were called this because speaking their names aloud was considered a violation of the sanctity of the festival due to the secrecy of the Mysteries.

Day Four—Epidauria. On the 18th the mystai retire from public life and spend the day indoors. During his life, Asclepius—a mortal son of Apollon who became a God of healing—was initiated into the Mysteries. He had arrived in Athens late on the 4th day and the rites of the first four days had to be rushed to accommodate him. After he became a God, he had a festival in Athens on the 4th day of the Mysteries which was named after his main temple in Epidauros. The festival included a procession with women carrying offerings to him, followed by a banquet with a special couch set aside for the God.

Day 5—Procession. On the 19th the myrtle-garlanded pilgrims gather between the Sacred Gate and the Dipylon Gate in the Kerameikos in Athens. Participants carry *bakchoi*—the bundles of myrtle branches tied with strands of wool. Along with the mystai and initiates carrying offerings, the procession includes the priestesses carrying the Sacred

Things in the *kistai*. Members of the ancient clans of the Kerykes and Eumolpidai carry torches and wear decorated tunics with boots. A statue of Dionysus under the name Iakchos leads the procession. He is *Ploutodotas*—the giver of wealth and was venerated at Eleusis with Demeter and Kore (Persephone.)

They set out along the Sacred Way, the fourteen mile winding road that leads to Eleusis. Songs rise from the crowd, punctuated with shouts of "Iakch' o Iakche!" Stopping here and there at all the shrines

Relief of the Great Eleusinian Mysteries
Demeter, Triptolemos and Persephone

to many Gods along the road, the sounds of the sacred procession—of flute, lyre and voice—echo through the hills.

As they pass the Rhetoi stream into the territory of Eleusis, the mystai are met by the descendants of the legendary king Krokos. They bind the right hand and left leg of each mystes with yellow ribbon. At another bridge over the Kephisos further on, men with their heads covered sit on the bridge and insult the priests and mystai as they cross.

Night falls and torches are lit to lead the way at last to Eleusis. When they arrive, the mystai are presented with *kernoi*—offering bowls with many small cups attached.

Day 6—Rites. On the 20th the mystai attend sacrifices to the Two Goddesses as well as to other Gods. There is a massive offering of grain meal to Demeter—enough to feed 1000. The mystai take part in the story—as Demeter fasted, the mystai fast. As she grieved, they grieve. As she abstained from wine, they also abstain. As she broke her fast, so do they, with the *kykeon*—the drink of water, barley meal and mint or pennyroyal described in the Homeric hymn. Presumably they also are reunited with Kore, sharing in the joy as well as the suffering of the Goddess.

Drinking the kykeon is an essential step in the Mysteries and the drink may have been entheogenic. There are several possible plants that would have entheogenic effects which were available in the region but the simplest and most likely is ergot, which grows on barley.

Day 7—Initiations. The 21st are the rituals in the Telesterion. Of all the richly-garbed priests descended from the ancient kings, the hierophant was central on this day. Chaste during the festival, only he can enter the inner sanctuary of the Anaktoron and only he can reveal the *hiera*—the Holy Things in the kistai boxes. To see them is the pinnacle of the initiation rite, but knowledge of the Sacred Items has been lost to time.

The mystai enter the Telesterion for initiation, stating as passwords that they have fasted, have drunk the kykeon, have taken from the kiste and after working it have put it back in the kalathos (basket.) Within the temple there are secret rites, the three unrepeatables:

dromena—things done

legomena—things said

and *deiknumena*—things revealed.

The myth of Demeter and Kore is reenacted, a gong is struck and there is deep darkness before the hierophant comes with lightning brightness from the Anaktoron. He carries the hiera and reveals them into the light, reciting the secret words as he holds up each object.

After the initiations, the mystai go to the Rharian Field for the *Pannychis*—a feast lasting through the rest of the night. North of Eleusis, this field is where the Athenians held that grain was first sown. There the blessed initiates sacrifice a bull, feast and tread the holy ground with dances.

Initiates of the prior year stay in the Telesterion for the final part of the ritual in which the final *mysteria* is revealed. An ear of grain is presented and reaped in silence.

Day 8—the Plemochoi. On the 22nd the initiates take special jars called plemochoi and tip them out to East and West. This might be a libation for the dead or an offering to bring rain.

Day 9—On the 23rd the initiates return home. The clothing worn during initiation is now sacred and the new initiates might either dedicate it to the Two Goddesses or take it home to use as swaddling blankets for newborns.

Happy is he among men upon earth who has seen these mysteries; but he who is uninitiate and who has no part in them, never has lot of like good things once he is dead, down in the darkness and gloom.

–Homeric Hymn to Demeter, tr. Hugh Evelyn-White, 1914

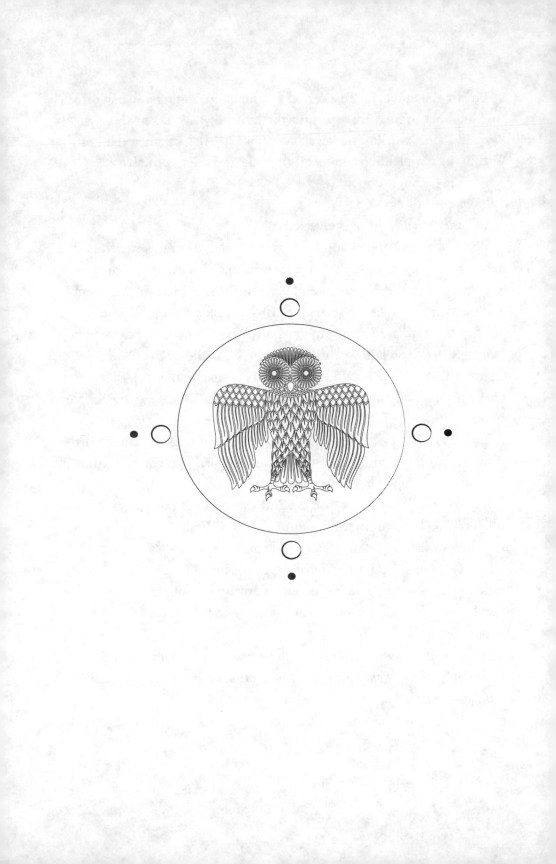

Pyanepsion
October

As farmers prepare the soil for sowing, there are three more festivals for Demeter this month. The first is the tithe on the 5th, then Demeter and Kore are honored in the Stenia. The Thesmophoria two days later is a major festival, but is strictly a women's festival, as most rites of Demeter were—the Mysteries are the exception. The version described here is Athenian, but the holiday was celebrated across Greece, likely with similar rites. The two other major festivals this month are the Oscophori—the winemaking celebration for Dionysus—and the Apaturia, celebrated by the phratrai. On the last day of the month, the loom is set up to weave the peplos for the Panathenaia. The rhythm of the festivals and their interrelation is easily seen in the festivals of

Pyanepsion—Thesmophoria was a completion of the action of the Skirophorion in the previous Spring, and the Chalkeia a necessary precursor to the following year's Panathenaia.

The Pyanepsia, Theseia and Oscophoria are all related to the myth of Theseus, the legendary King of Athens who sailed to the palace of Minos on Crete, navigated the labyrinth of Daedalus and slaughtered the minotaur. He did this to stop the bloody tribute of seven young men and seven women from Athens being sent periodically to be devoured by the monster. These festivals focus on specific aspects of his return journey—the Pyanepsia on his votive sacrifices, the Theseia on the hero's return and the Oscophoria on Dionysus, who rescued Ariadne after Theseus abandoned her on the island of Naxos.

In addition to the focus on Theseus, there is a sacrifice to the Heroines in Erchia. These rites recall that human action and stories impact the world and are worth celebrating along with the divine. Take note of the following dates:

5th of the month: Proerosia, a tithe to Demeter in Eleusis

7th of the month: Pyanepsia, a festival in Eleusis for Pythian Apollon

8th of the month: Theseia, an Athenian festival in honor of the hero Theseus

8th of the month: Oscophoria, an Attic winemaking festival in honor of Dionysus

9th of the month: Stenia, a minor Athenian festival for Demeter and Persephone

11th–13th of the month: Thesmophoria, an Athenian women's festival for Demeter

14th of the month: a sacrifice to the Heroines by the Attic town of Erchia

19th–21st of the month: Apaturia, a festival for the phratrai

30th of the month: Chalkeia, an Athenian festival for Athena and Hephaestus

Proerosia

There was a story in ancient times of a plague came to Greece. The pestilence covered the land so that all cities suffered. Apollon was the God who could both send and alleviate plague, and so the Athenians did what they always did in times of fear and desperation—they sent messengers to Delphi to consult the Oracle of Apollon there. The messengers went back to the dark recesses of the temple where the priestess called the Pythia sat writhing in her tripod, inhaling the vapor that arose from the stream that ran beneath the temple. Once the priests interpreted the message delivered from the God through the Pythia, the oracle told the Athenians to sacrifice to Demeter. This was to be done not just for themselves, but on behalf of all Greek people and cities. They were also to ensure that all cities sent tithes of wheat and barley to the Goddess at Eleusis. In historic times, farmers in Attica sent one part of every six hundred of their barley crops and one part of every twelve hundred of their wheat crops as a tithe to Eleusis. In the years when the power of Athens was great, she compelled all the cities she commanded to tithe in the same way and invited all other Greek cities to do the same to prevent further plagues from arising in the future.

On the 5th of the month, a herald and the hierophant of Eleusis announced the Proerosia and invited offerings. The name of the festival—Proerosia—means "prior to plowing." By tithing first fruits of the prior crop to the Grain Goddess before beginning to plough and sow, the Athenians ensured the blessing of Demeter on the following year's crop while also averting further retribution. In later periods oxen were sacrificed as well.

Excerpts from the Orphic Hymn to Demeter (Ceres)

Goddess of seed, of fruits abundant, fair,
Harvest and threshing, are thy constant care.
Who dwellest in Eleusinia's seats retired,
Lovely, delightful queen, by all desired.
Nurse of all mortals, whose benignant mind,
First ploughing oxen to the yoke confined
And gave to men, what nature's wants require,
With plenteous means of bliss which all desire.
Rejoicing in the reapers sickles, kind,
Whose nature lucid, earthly, pure, we find.
A car with dragons yoked, 'tis thine to guide,
And orgies singing round thy throne to ride.
Only-begotten, much-producing queen,
All flowers are thine and fruits of lovely green.
Bright Goddess, come, with Summer's
rich increase
Swelling and pregnant, leading smiling Peace.

—tr. Thomas Taylor, 1792, spelling modernized by M. Borden

Pyanepsia

The greatest oracle of the Greek world was Delphi, where the priestess of Apollon, the Pythia, would sit in the tripod and convey the wise words of the Gods to all pilgrims. The oracle was sacred to all and held great sway over the Greek cities. The sanctuary lies in a sheltered spot at the foot of Mount Parnassus, but this valley did not always belong to Apollon.

In a mountain stream near rocky Parnassus there was a fierce, bloated python, a monstrous dragon. She loved to eat both sheep and shepherds. When Hera bore the monster Typhon in revenge on Zeus for birthing Athena himself, she gave her ghastly son to this cruel creature to raise and she taught him all her wicked ways. Every person who had approached the thing was devoured by it. None could overcome such a beast, until Phoebus Apollon came to its lair to bring it to its death.

After Apollon was born on Delos, he was fed nectar and ambrosia in place of mother's milk. On tasting the divine food, Phoebus spoke in a clear voice and claimed the bow and the lyre to himself, and said that he would give prophecies to humankind so that they would know the will of Zeus. The God with long hair, the far shooter began to walk, carrying his silver bow across mountains and groves. The son of Leto, clothed in the sweet-scented garments of the immortal Gods, sped to Olympus. There Apollon plays his lyre, stepping lightly among the Gods and delighting them all.

From there the far-shooting son of Zeus and Leto began to wander across all Earth, searching for the place to set his oracle. When he came to the spring of Telphusa, the lovely grove seemed the perfect spot and he began to lay the foundations of his temple.

But the Goddess of those waters did not love the sounds of trampling hooves or the lapping of mules as they refreshed themselves. She asked him to find another spot and recommended a glade at the foot of Mount Parnassus. And so Phoebus went to that place where the cliff hangs over and decided to build his temple there. He declared that his would be an oracle for all people and that he would guide them unfailingly.

That valley was the place where the python lurked, so Phoebus brought death from afar, shooting the monster with his arrows. She writhed, balking at her doom, and as blood trickled out of her mouth, the God stood proudly over her and boasted that she who had brought so much death was now laid out to rot in the Sun. Helios swiftly broke down her body and as the monster decayed, Apollon grew in power and took the name Pythian. Realizing that the stream Telphusa had tried to trick him by leading him there, he covered her spring with rocks, raised his altar and took her holy name for his own, so he is called Telphusian as well.

When the hero Theseus stopped at Delos—the island of Apollon's birth—he pledged there that if he and his crew returned safely to Athens, he would offer seeds, grains and beans to Apollon. He returned

Zeus combatting Typhon

on the 7th of Pyanepsion and so the festival was instituted by him. The name of the feast was Pyanepsia, which means "boiling beans." Pythian Apollon, the God of the great oracle, was honored in Eleusis on the seventh as he was born on the seventh. The oracle at Delphi was the origin of the Proerosia tithing festival two days earlier and this holiday may be a sort of thanksgiving to him for instituting that offering of first fruits. During the festival, the city made offerings to Pythian Apollon and set a table with a meal for him. One of the main dishes was made of beans and grains cooked together, called *panspermia*.

Hymns to Helios and to the Horai—Goddesses of the seasons who mark the passage of time—were sung at this festival. One of the events was the *eiresione*. This is the name of an olive or laurel branch wrapped in wool. It had fruits tied to it as well as branches, harps and a cup all made of pastry attached as well. A boy with both parents still living processed with it and set it at the entrance to the temple. In Athens, boys carried these branches from door to door on the day of the festival, singing songs of begging. Set up by the door of the house, the eiresione could bless a home with good fortune all year.

Iliad, Book 1, lines 471-474

So the whole day long they sought to appease the god with song, singing the beautiful paean, the sons of the Achaeans, hymning the god who works from afar; and his heart was glad, as he heard.

—tr. A.T. Murray, 1924

Theseia

Poseidon blessed Minos, the great king of Knossos on Crete, sending him a perfect bull that arose out of the waves. Minos was greedy and instead of offering this perfect sacrifice to the God, he kept it to serve as a sire in his herd and so enrich himself. He was punished, though, when it also served as a sire for his wife, who was struck by the God with an unnatural lust for the beast. She bore the minotaur, the half-man, half-bull proof of Minos' impiety. Unwilling to bring on himself the blood guilt that would surely come from slaying the creature, the king of the most powerful state in the Aegean at that time determined to hide it. He hired the inventor Daedalus to fashion a trap for it, and the crafty man designed the labyrinth. The creature's lowing could be heard echoing in the halls of the palace, so Minos began to send the children of his enemies into the labyrinth to keep the minotaur fed and entertained.

Athens owed tribute to Minos at that time, and every nine years the city sent seven young men and seven maidens to Crete as tribute for the labyrinth. One year came when the prince of the city volunteered to go as tribute. Although Athenian tradition also held him to be a son of Poseidon, the tale goes that Theseus was the child of King Aegeus of Athens. Aegeus had slept with the wife of the king of Troezen, and told her that if she became pregnant, she should raise their child. He showed her where he had buried his sword and sandals, so that if the child were a boy it could retrieve them when he came of age and his true father could recognize him by those signs. She bore a son and named him Theseus. When he was old enough, he took his father's possessions and set out for Athens, overcoming many dangers on the way. When he arrived in Athens, he was immediately

Theseus battling the Minotaur

recognized not by the king, but by the king's wicked wife, Medea the sorceress. She intended for her own sons to take the throne one day, and attempted to poison Theseus when he came to the court of Aegeus as a visitor. The king knew his wife intended to serve the youth poisoned wine, and was not concerned—he knew the woman he'd married but did not know that he had a son, much less what his name might be, and his wife had convinced him that the handsome young man might be a threat to his power. But as Theseus lifted the cup to his lips, the king's eye happened to pass over his young guest's sword. Recognizing it immediately, he knocked the cup out of his hand and publicly claimed him as his son and heir right then and there. At this, the brother and nephews of Aegeus drew swords and rose up, hoping to take the throne for themselves. Theseus killed them all in the melee that followed, proving his worth as a warrior.

When the time came for the tribute to Knossos, Theseus volunteered and set sail for Crete with Minos in the black-sailed ship. Before he left, he'd told Aegeus privately of his plan to try to kill the minotaur and bring an end to the bloody tribute and he'd sworn to return, saying he would come with white sails on the ship to show his triumph. While they were at sea, King Minos molested one of the Athenian maidens and was stopped by Theseus when he heard the girl crying for help. Minos then raised his arms to the sky, praying to his father Zeus to send a sign that he was truly his son. Lightning flashed across the clouds over the ship, confirming his claim. But Theseus was also said to be a son of a God, so Minos challenged him, throwing a ring overboard into the black waves, telling the boy that if he were really the child of Poseidon, he would be able to fetch it. Theseus dove into the sea and disappeared beneath the water, to the grief of all the Athenians onboard the ship. While they waited—sure that he had drowned but unable to tear themselves from the rail—dolphins carried the young hero to Poseidon's palace, where his father's wife Amphitrite decked him out in purple robes and a wreath of roses. He arose out of the sea in all this raiment, and in this way the hero arrived at Knossos.

The radiant young prince seduced the king's daughter Ariadne into helping him survive the labyrinth. She gave him the secret of the thread to find his way and stored a sword in the labyrinth for him, so that he could have some hope of besting the monster that lurked within. This creature was, of course the girl's brother. Once Theseus slew the minotaur, he quickly fled Knossos to gain a lead on the swift ships that Minos would surely send to follow them. He had taken Ariadne with him as he'd promised, but had no further desire to fulfill his oaths to her. The Athenians stopped to rest on the island of Naxos, the birthplace of Dionysus. From there the ship slipped away by night, leaving the girl still sleeping on the sand. She awoke in confusion, unable to believe that her lover had abandoned her, and wandered the island in grief until Dionysus himself comforted her, and she became his wife.

Ariadne's confusion led her into the arms of the God and eternal glory, but Theseus, too, was confused. In his rush to return home, he forgot to change the ship's sails to white. His father Aegeus stood on the cliffs, looking out over the sea for some sign of the ship. When he saw a black sail break the horizon, he threw himself to his death, and so the sea bears his name. Theseus returned from slaying the minotaur as a king on the seventh of Pyanepsion.

Theseus was a good king and a legend arose in later times that he was a man of the people and had established democracy while king but that the state reverted back to monarchy after his death. He had a small hero cult in the archaic period, but in the 5th century BCE the oracle of Delphi told the Athenians that Theseus died on the island of Scyros, and that his bones should be returned to Athens and a more robust cult of Theseus should be established. This was an excellent opportunity for conquest, so Athens conquered Scyros, brought remains back to the city and instituted the Theseia festival in the early king's honor on the eighth of Pyanepsion. It was not the seventh because the eighth of every month is Poseidon's day and because the seventh was the day that Theseus learned of the death of his father Aegeus. In addition to a procession, the festival included a sacrifice and athletic contests. There was a feast with meat given to the people of the city, served with milk porridge. Like at the Panathenaia, there were competitions of manly excellence, races, torch races and many other of the same events.

Athenian legends paint king Minos as a tyrant, but after he died Zeus appointed him as a judge in the Underworld.

Oschophoria

When Theseus returned to Athens from Crete, first he made sacrifices to the Gods as he had promised. Immediately afterward, he heard the announcement of the death of his father Aegeus, strangely mixed to Theseus' ears with the joyous cries of the Oschophoria festival that was being celebrated on that day.

The major festivals of Dionysus are later in the year, but this one celebrates the wine harvest and the production of wine. Even in modern Greece, the grape harvest is a joyous occasion where people gather together to harvest and press grapes at this time of year. Wherever there is wine, there is Dionysus, because he is in the vine itself.

The myths of Dionysus are as straightforward as his circling, winding grapevines. Even ancient historians speculated that there may have been more than one God with this name. Dionysus—frequently called *Bakchos* by the Greeks—has at least three stories of his birth, all fragmentary. The Homeric Hymns call him the son of Zeus and Semele, giving him the title "the insewn" as he was carried to term in the thigh of Zeus. The Orphic tradition is that he is a son of Zeus and Persephone or Zeus and Demeter. Zeus joined with Persephone in the form of a snake and she birthed the horned boy Zagreus. The child was so powerful that Hera feared he might overtake the prowess of her own children and so she plotted with the Titans against him. Distracting the baby with his own reflection in a mirror, the Titans cut him into many pieces. They boiled his corpse but Demeter managed to steal enough of it to rebirth him as Dionysus. In another version Zeus himself found the boy's heart, mixed it up with wine and gave it to the princess Semele. By drinking it, she became pregnant with the child, but Hera still plotted against him. She tricked Semele into convincing Zeus to show her his divine form, which killed her. Then Zeus took the child from Semele's dead womb and sewed him into his own thigh to carry to term. In yet another form of the tale, Semele dreamed of carrying a bull-shaped child before Zeus came to her in the form of a snake and the conception of Dionysus filled the room with vines, fruit and foliage.

None of the Gods are simple and all have many sides to their personalities and many faces they might show. The two primary depictions of Bakchos are of a bearded man who might or might not be wild-looking and a beardless young man who was both beautiful and effeminate. He might also have horns—as many Gods do in their images—but the myths also whisper about his bull's shape. He was at times rumored to be a foreign God even though he is one of the oldest, with his name appearing in Mycenaean Linear B tablets. The mystery of his birth aside, all the stories of Dionysus agree that he sets his worshippers free—sometimes too free. He is called *Eleutherios*, the great liberator, and wine is his primary vehicle. He lightens hearts, bringing joy and song with him and wherever he goes people find their feet twisting like the grapevine in dance.

In the ancient celebration, the people processed from a shrine of Dionysus in Athens to a shrine of Athena Skiras in the nearby town

Roman mosaic depicting Dionysus and a musician

of Phaleron. There was also a shrine of Demeter there, connecting the rites of Dionysus to the Skira festival of early summer. The procession itself centered around two young men dressed in women's clothing who carried *oschoi*—grape vine branches laden with fruit. The youths were chosen from the upper-class families of Athens and represented the young soldiers Theseus snuck into Minos' hall dressed as girls. Women followed behind them in the parade, carrying all the food for the banquet besides the sacrificial animals. Chosen by lot, these women reenacted the part of the mothers of the child sacrifices sent to the Cretan minotaur in the story of Theseus. The mothers would carry down to the port at Piraeus a last home-cooked meal to their children as they waited on ships to depart to their deaths. After the sacrifice in Phaleron, the people shouted out, "Eleleu Iou Iou," which expressed a sense of triumph in the first part and confusion in the second, echoing Theseus' confusion on hearing the festival songs and the cries of grief for his father mixed together.

Orphic Hymn to Dionysus, 1–10

Bacchus I call, loud-sounding and divine,
Fanatic God, a two-fold shape is thine:
Thy various names and attributes I sing,
O, first-born, thrice begotten, Bacchic king:
Rural, ineffable, two-formed, obscure,
Two-horned, with ivy crowned, howling,[1] pure.
Bull-faced, and martial, bearer of the vine,
Endued with counsel prudent and divine:
Triennial, whom the leaves of vines adorn,
Of Jove and Proserpine, occultly born.

–tr. Thomas Taylor , 1792

---

1   M. Borden changed Taylor's untranslated Greek term *euion* to "howling" and modernized spelling for clarity

Stenia and Thesmophoria

The Stenia and Thesmophoria are women's festivals in honor of Demeter and Persephone. At the Stenia two days before the larger festival, women gathered at night. The rites included sitting on the ground and ritualized insults and coarse joking between the worshippers. These feature in many of the rites of Demeter, including the Thesmophoria. They re-enact the part of Demeter's myth in which she refuses to sit on the couch offered to her and cannot be cheered up from her grief until the servant Iambe tells her these sorts of mocking jokes.

The Thesmophoria was part of the religious and magical preparation for sowing crops. Three months earlier at the Skira festival—another women's festival for Demeter—women placed sacrificial objects in caves. Temples of Demeter often had caves below or close by, and in that rite, the worshippers placed sacrificed piglets as well as models of snakes and phalluses made of dough into these caverns. Pigs were a usual sacrifice to Demeter, snakes are associated with all chthonic activities and the phalluses are obvious fertility emblems. In the three-day festival of Thesmophoria, these offerings were retrieved to bless the fields as preparation for sowing.

Day 1—Ascent. On 11th Pyanepsion, women processed to the festival site. They worked together to build huts and set up campsites as they were to remain there for two nights. The name of the day probably comes from the tendency of temples of Demeter to be situated on hills.

Day 2—The Fast. On 12th Pyanepsion, the worshippers sat on the ground and did not eat any solid food. They insulted one

another, told jokes about sex and hit each other with a whip made of braided bark. For the men who remained in Athens, no official legal business was conducted on this day.

Day 3—Day of Fair Offspring. The day of the 13th began as soon as night fell—what modern readers would think of as the evening before. Once it was dark, the Antletriai descended into the caves. These were women who had been chosen for the sacred duty of carrying out the sacrificial remains from the Skira. They had abstained from sex for three days prior. The Antletriai went into the caves, clapping and making noise to scare away the snakes that lived in them. They brought up the rotten remains and placed them on the altars of Demeter and Persephone, because the putrid mess was now consecrated to the Two Goddesses. Everyone carried home some of it to sow with their winter wheat at the end of the month, making their fields magically fertile and actually adding nutrients as well. In Greek, the name of this day—*Kalligenia* (fair offspring)—is associated with Demeter and particularly with her rulership of the fertility of humans as well as the fields. Women feasted on pomegranates and pork and offered cakes shaped like genitals to the Gods. Virgins could not attend this festival, and this day most likely included a ritual, sacrifice or blessing for the personal fertility of the worshippers present.

The putrefied remains of the sacrifice were sown with the seeds because people believed they caused the fields to be especially fertile. It is probable that they actually had this effect. *The Odyssey* mentions piles of manure maturing before being put on the fields, so the ancient Greeks were well aware of the process and benefits of composting. This rite sacralizes the process and views it as an expression of the agricultural power of death to bring life—the power of the Two Goddesses, Demeter and Persephone.

From the Orphic Hymn to Persephone

O, vernal queen, whom grassy plains delight,
Sweet to the smell, and pleasing to the sight,
Whose holy form in budding fruits we view,
Earth's vigorous offspring of a various hue.
Espoused in Autumn, life and death alone
To wretched mortals from thy power is known.
For thine the task according to thy will,
Life to produce, and all that lives to kill.
Hear, blessed Goddess, send a rich increase
Of various fruits from earth, with lovely Peace.
Send Health with gentle hand,
and crown my life
With blest abundance, free from noisy strife.
Last in extreme old age the prey of Death,
Dismiss we willing to the realms beneath.
To thy fair palace, and the blissful plains
Where happy spirits dwell, and Pluto reigns.

—tr. Thomas Taylor, 1792,
spelling modernized by M. Borden

Apaturia

Greek cities had brotherhoods called phratriai. The male membership considered themselves descendants of the same distant ancestors. Each brotherhood celebrated the three-day Apaturia during Pyanepsion on the date they chose. The first day—called Dinner—consisted of gathering for a ritual evening meal. The second day—called Sacrifice—included sacrifices to Zeus Phratrios and Athena Phratria. The third day was the Day of Youths for registering infants born in the last year into the phratria.

Men made sacrifices with the phratria on the Apaturia following a male child's birth and again when that child came of age. They could also offer sacrifices at the Apaturia to celebrate a marriage. Given all the revelry on the third day, naturally the fourth was set aside for recovery and was called the Morning After.

Chalkeia

Theogony lines 924–928, by Hesiod

*Zeus himself gave birth from his own head to bright-eyed Tritogeneia,
the awful, the strife-stirring, the host-leader, the unwearying, the queen,
who delights in tumults and wars and battles. But Hera without union
with Zeus—for she was very angry and quarrelled with her mate—bare
famous Hephaestus, who is skilled in crafts more than all the sons of
Heaven.*

–tr. Hugh Evelyn-White, 1914

So great are the king and queen of Olympus that each created a child
without another parent. These children, Athena and Hephaestus,
are also the two Gods of crafts. Hephaestus is a metalworker and
Athena a weaver, as attested in the well-known story of the contest
with Arachne before the Goddess turns her into a spider. They were
associated with each other and Athens had one of the few temples
of Hephaestus in Greece. He was also honored alongside Athena at
the festival of the Chalkeia.

The Greek word for copper is *chalkos* and the closely-related
chalkeis means smith. These words gave the festival its name.
It was an important occasion for metalworkers, but also for all
craftsmen—spinners, weavers, vase painters, potters, jewelers
and the makers of all other crafts celebrated this day by carrying
baskets of grain offerings in procession and making offerings to
the Gods. These offerings were made to Athena as the founder—
Archegetis and to Athena *Ergane*—the worker. This aspect of the
Goddess was ancient—Athena was honored by the Mycenaean
kings because textile manufacturing was an important part of the
Mycenaean economy.

This was the day when the priestess of Athena set up a loom on the Acropolis to weave a peplos for Athena. She was helped by specially chosen young girls called arrephoroi and by the ergastinai—the women who would labor for the next nine months on the peplos which they would present to the Goddess at the Panathenaia.

Homeric Hymn to Hephaestus

Sing, clear-voiced Muse, of Hephaestus famed for inventions. With bright-eyed Athena he taught men glorious crafts throughout the world, men who before used to dwell in caves in the mountains like wild beasts. But now that they have learned crafts through Hephaestus the famed worker, easily they live a peaceful life in their own houses the whole year round.

Be gracious, Hephaestus, and grant me success and prosperity!

–tr. Hugh Evelyn–White, 1914

Maimakterion
November

Pyanepsion is the last month of Summer and Maimakterion the first of the Winter season. There are no significant festivals this month and trade by sea and agricultural activity also slow down. The name of the month comes from an epithet of Zeus meaning "blustering," and it is fitting. Greece—and Athens in particular—shifts rapidly from being breathtakingly hot with not a cloud for months to being regularly and sometimes continually drenched with cold rain. The chill damp is not hospitable festival weather as sacrifices and other festival events took place almost exclusively outdoors.

Because months are named after festivals, there was likely an early festival called the Maimakteria this month, but information about it has not survived. This month would be a fitting time to offer to Zeus as the God of Storms to minimize the impact of winter storms on the household. There is evidence of the Pompaia, a ritual of purification by the priests of Athens. The following festivals occurred at unclear dates during this month:

Maimakteria, a possible feast for Zeus of Blustering Storms

Pompaia, a purification rite of Zeus Meilichios

Pompaia

Pompaia means "procession" and the main activity of this festival was a procession of the priests of Zeus. Unlike most other festivals, ordinary citizens had no part of this rite. The priests carried the *Dion Koidion*, a sheepskin associated with Zeus *Meilichios* (the friendly one,) a chthonic Zeus who appeared as a snake. This was the skin of a sheep that had been sacrificed to the God. A person was purified by standing on it with the left foot. In addition to the Dion Koidion, the priests carried the caduceus of Hermes—a wand wrapped with twining snakes. These two magical objects had great power to ward off any evil or ill luck and by processing with them the priesthood protected the city from the many misfortunes the untrustworthy winter season could bring.

Zeus Meilichios is considered a God of purification, especially from the miasma of bloodshed. The ancient Greeks were deeply concerned with defilement. Physical dirt could be washed away by pure water but the touch of death was not so easily removed. When a family member died, the survivors were unclean and only after a set period of time could the household be purified again. The worst sort of defilement came from murder and this blood guilt could only be cleansed by blood which was shed in a sacred manner, from holy sacrifice because blood was defilement and also purification. The classic example of blood guilt is Orestes, who was driven mad by the tormenting Furies sent from the Underworld by his murdered mother. Apollon himself cleansed him through sacrifice—the hero stood under the pig and when the God cut its throat, he was washed of polluting blood by being bathed in sacrificial blood. One of the many shrines of Zeus Meilichios in Athens was at the spot where Theseus cleansed himself of blood guilt in legend.

Orphic Fragment, To Zeus

Zeus is the first. Zeus the thunderer is the last.
Zeus is the head. Zeus is the middle and by Zeus
all things were fabricated.
Zeus is male, Immortal Zeus is female.
Zeus is the foundation of the earth and of the
starry heaven.
Zeus is the breath of all things. Zeus is the rushing
of indefatigable fire.
Zeus is the root of the sea. He is the
Sun and Moon.
Zeus is the king. He is the author of
universal life:

One Power, one Daemon, the mighty prince
of all things.
One kingly frame, in which this
universe revolves,
Fire and water, earth and ether, night and day,
And Metis (Counsel) the primeval father, and
all-delightful Eros (Love.)
All these things are United in the vast
body of Zeus.
Would you behold his head and his fair face,
It is the resplendent heaven, round which
his golden locks
Of glittering stars are beautifully exalted in the air.
On each side are the two golden taurine horns,
The risings and settings, the tracks of the
celestial gods.

His eyes the sun and the Opposing moon,
His unfallacious Mind the royal incorruptible
Ether.

–tr. I. P. Cory, 1832

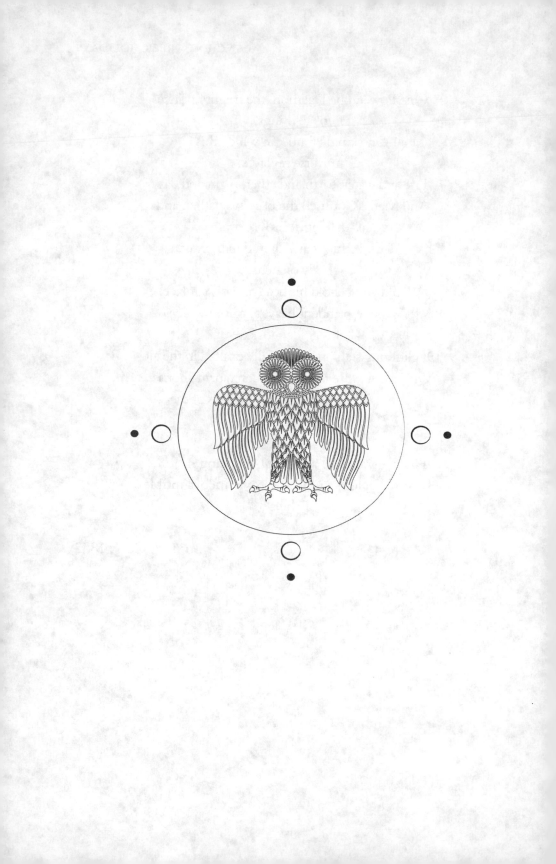

Poseideon
December

Because of the name of the month, there was probably once a festival for Poseidon at this time of year. The 8th of every month is dedicated to him, so it is appropriate to honor the Earthshaker on the 8th day of the month named after him. There was little seafaring at this time of year, but the sea would have been especially difficult to navigate and the dangerous power of the God quite evident.

The notable festivals this month are the Haloa for Dionysus and Demeter and the Country Dionysia. Both were associated with license and were phallic in nature. The name of the Plerosia on the 5th is related to the word for "full" so it was most likely a sacrifice to Demeter or Zeus in thanks for a good harvest or in anticipation of the next agricultural cycle. Erchia sacrificed to Zeus Horios on the 16th. This epithet means Zeus of the Boundaries and under this name, Zeus—ever the keeper of order—protected the boundary stones. His cult was managed by the descendants of Kerykes, the same family who served as priests of Eleusis. Take note of the following dates:

5th of the month: Plerosia, a festival in the Attic town of Myrrhinus

8th of the month: Poseidea, an Athenian festival for Poseidon

16th of the month: a sacrifice to Zeus Horios by the Attic town of Erchia

19th of the month: a private sacrifice to the Wind Gods in Athens

26th of the month: Haloa, a festival of Demeter and Dionysus at Eleusis in Attica

During the second half of the month: Country Dionysia, a rural Attic festival for Dionysus

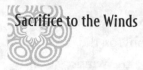

Sacrifice to the Winds

Hesiod's Theogony, lines 869-880

And from Typhoeus come boisterous winds which blow damply, except Notus and Boreas and clear Zephyr. These are a god-sent kind, and a great blessing to men; but the others blow fitfully upon the sea. Some rush upon the misty sea and work great havoc among men with their evil, raging blasts; for varying with the season they blow, scattering ships and destroying sailors. And men who meet these upon the sea have no help against the mischief. Others again over the boundless, flowering earth spoil the fair fields of men who dwell below, filling them with dust and cruel uproar.

—tr. Hugh Evelyn-White, 1914

From the earliest days, the Greeks understood that Wind could be both benevolent and destructive, so it was particularly important to propitiate the kindly Wind powers, especially in the more difficult seasons. On the 19th of Poseideon there was a sacrifice to the Winds done privately rather than by the state. There were quite a few Wind Gods, but the most

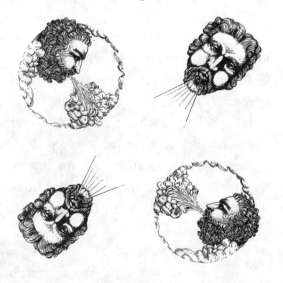

important were the Anemoi who represented the winds of the cardinal directions: Euros the East, Notos the South, Zephyros the West and Boreas the North. There were hymns and prayers to the winds as well as sacrifices. Three of the Winds have prayers in the Orphic Hymns.

Orphic Hymn to the West Wind

Sea-born, aerial, blowing from the west,
Sweet gales, who give to wearied labour rest,
Vernal and grassy, and of gentle found,
To ships delightful, through the sea profound,
For these, impelled by you with gentle force,
Pursue with prosperous Fate their
destined course.
With blameless gales regard my suppliant prayer,
Zephyrs unseen, light-winged, and
formed from air.

–tr. Thomas Taylor, 1792,
spelling modernized by M. Borden

Orphic Hymn to the South Wind

Wide coursing gales, whose lightly leaping feet
With rapid wings the air's wet bosom beat,
Approach benevolent, swift-whirling powers,
With humid clouds the principles of flowers,
For flowery clouds are portioned to your care,
To send on earth from all surrounding air.
Bear, blessed powers, these holy rites attend,
And fruitful rains on earth all-parent send.

–tr. Thomas Taylor, 1792,
spelling modernized by M. Borden

Orphic Hymn to the North Wind

Boreas, whose wintry blasts, terrific, tear
The bosom of the deep surrounding air,
Cold icy power, approach, and favoring blow,
And Thrace a while desert exposed to snow:
The misty station of the air dissolve,
With pregnant clouds, whose frames in showers
resolve,
Serenely temper all within the sky,
And wipe from moisture, Aether's beauteous eye.

–tr. Thomas Taylor, 1792,
spelling modernized by M. Borden

Haloa

The Haloa was a secret women's festival at Eleusis. A *halos* is a threshing floor, but this festival did not fall during the grain harvest. The festival carried an association with sexual license and adultery typical of festivals of Dionysus, and it likely had a fertility theme as most festivals of Demeter did. Uniting these themes, an image associated with Haloa shows a woman scattering grain on phalluses set upright in the soil.

In the festival, men prepared a feast and then departed, leaving the women to enjoy the banquet. There was wine as well as a great deal of food, including cakes shaped like genitals. Certain foods forbidden at the mysteries were not allowed at this festival either: birds, eggs, fish, pomegranates and apples.

Woman tending to a garden of phalli
set upright in the ground

The participants carried models of genitalia (both male and female) and the priestesses whispered in the womens' ears that they should sleep with people other than their husbands. They engaged in the usual exchange of crude jokes and insults. The celebration had a reputation for being orgiastic and was associated with prostitutes.

From Aristophanes' *The Frogs*

Now raise ye another [hymn]
To the Queen of the Fruits of the Earth.
To Demeter the Corn-giver, Goddess
and Mother,
Make worship in musical mirth.
Approach, O Queen of orgies pure,
And us, thy faithful band, ensure
From morn to eve to ply secure
Our mocking and our clowning:
To grace thy feast with many a hit
Of merry jest or serious wit,
And laugh, and earn the prize, and flit
Triumphant to the crowning.

—tr. Gilbert Murray, 1912

Country Dionysia

During the second half of Poseideon, each village celebrated the Country Dionysia at whatever time they chose, as long as it was in the second half of the month. Lighthearted in nature, this midwinter festival brightens the colder, darker seasons with the pleasure of sex and its inherent promise of Spring.

The procession was as loud as the howling God, dithyrambs and priapic songs punctuating the laughter and calls of the ivy-garlanded participants. The girl with the barley basket went first, but what everyone was waiting for was the large, wooden phallus that was invoked and then paraded through the streets. Others followed with many offerings: loaf carriers, wine carriers and water carriers. There was fruit in a basket and a male goat dragged along for the sacrifice.

Satyr and Dionysus

All could attend, even slaves, and participate in the games that followed the parade: trying to stand on top of an inflated goatskin covered with grease, one-footed tag, one-footed races, and contests of who could hop on one foot the most times. There were more formal competitions as well, of singing and dancing. No festival of Dionysus is complete without drama, and both comedies and tragedies were performed, both designed to intensify the emotions. The festival was playful and it was also carnal— wine and sex were everywhere, the Great Liberator's promise of freedom felt first in the flesh.

From the Epigrams of Meleager of Gadara

I shall bear, Bacchus, your boldness, I swear it by yourself. Lead on, begin the revel. You are a god—govern a mortal heart. Born in the flame, you love the flame that love has, and again you lead me, your suppliant, in bonds. Truly you are a traitor and faithless, and while you bid us hide your mysteries, you would now bring mine to light.

—tr. W.R. Paton, 1916

Gamelion
January

There are two minor Athenian festivals this month, the Lenaia for Dionysus and the Gamelia—also called the Theogamia—a festival honoring the marriage of Zeus and Hera. Because of this, Gamelion was the most popular month for marriage ceremonies.

There are three Erchian sacrifices this month. The first is to Apollon Apotropaeos—the averter of evil, Apollong Nymphegetes—leader of the Nymphs, and to the Nymphs. These are divinities of the land that take the form of young women. They are associated with many Olympian Gods, including Apollon. The second sacrifice at Erchia is to Athena. Late in the month there is a sacrifice to Kourotrophos, Hera, Teleius and Poseidon. The title Kourotrophos means "the one who raises boys" and many Gods who serve as protectors of children bear this epithet. Poseidon is God of the sea and earthquakes. Hera is the queen of the Gods and protector of marriage while Zeus Teleios is Zeus of the ceremony, meaning the marriage ceremony. These are connected to the festival of the Gamelia in Athens on the same day. Take note of the following dates:

8th of the month: a sacrifice to Apollon Apotropaeos, Apollon Nymphegetes and the Nymphs in the Attic town of Erchia

9th of the month: a sacrifice to Athena in the Attic town of Erchia

12th–15th of the month: Lenaia, an Athenian festival of Dionysus

27th of the month: a sacrifice to Kourotrophos, Hera, Zeus Teleios and Poseidon in Erchia

27th of the month: Gamelia, an Athenian celebration of the marriage of Zeus and Hera

Lenaia

In some cities, this month was called Lenaion after this festival of Dionysus. In Athens, the Lenaion was an early theater as well as a sanctuary of Dionysus. Theater originated with the worship of this God and was inextricably linked to it in ancient times. The Lenaia festival consisted of a series of plays that went on for several days. Dionysus was the God of theater and both comedies and tragedies were performed. The audience called out to the God as Iakchos Ploutodotas— the bringer of wealth. This connected the ritual to the Eleusinian Mysteries, where he was also called by that name.

The festival was only open to Athenians and as at other festivals of Dionysus, there was a procession with people riding in carts or floats while singing coarse songs. In images that might depict the Lenaia, there are women venerating a mask or head of Dionysus attached to a pole that has been dressed in clothing. Offering cakes hang from it as well. Women pour wine while others with flutes and tambourines dance with the *thyrsus*—the staff carried by Dionysus and his followers. While theater might have been the main focus of the festival, it is clear that where Bakchos goes, revelry follows.

The Maenads were female followers of Dionysus. They worshipped him by dancing, singing and drinking wine until they were in an ecstatic frenzy. Maenads set aside the typical conventions of society for these rites. Where Athenian women were usually fully covered and well-groomed, in worship as maenads they had free-flowing hair, wore animal skins and carried the phallic, pine-cone tipped thyrsus. Shouting euhoi, they spun in twirling dances and in their euphoric mania would eat raw meat and handle snakes and fire without being harmed. At the end of their ecstasy, they fell to the ground.

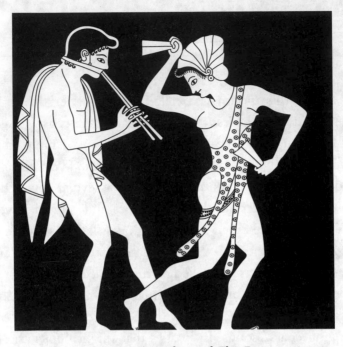

From Aristophanes' *The Frogs*

Now call the God of blooming mien,
Raise the mystic chorus.
Our comrade he and guide unseen,
With us and before us.
Iacchus high in glory…Iaccus, happy dancer,
be our guide.
Thyself, that poorest men thy joy should share,
Didst rend thy robe, thy royal sandal tear,
That feet unshod might dance, and
robes rent wide
Wave in thy revel with no after care.
Iacchus, happy dancer, be our guide.

—tr. Gilbert Murray, 1912

Gamelia

The Gamelia honoring the marriage of Zeus and Hera gave its name to this month but few details about the occasion survive. There are several myths of how the Gods came to be joined. In one tale Zeus transforms himself into a cuckoo to seduce Hera—she is shown in art with a bird in her lap. In another, Hera hides from Zeus and has to be talked into sleeping with him by a human. In the Iliad, Hera seduces Zeus and he confesses that he hadn't been so attracted to her since they were sleeping together secretly to avoid their disapproving parents. However it came about, their wedding feast lasted many years and the apples of the Hesperides were a wedding gift from their grandmother Gaia.

Iliad, book 14

Hera then went to…the topmost peak of Ida, and Zeus, driver of the clouds, set eyes upon her. As soon as he did so he became inflamed with the same passionate desire for her that he had felt when they had first enjoyed each other's embraces and slept with one another without their dear parents knowing anything about it. He went up to her and said, "What do you want that you have come hither from Olympus—and that too with neither chariot nor horses to convey you?"

Then Hera told him a lying tale and said, "I am going to the world's end, to visit Okeanos, from whom all we gods proceed, and mother Tethys…I have come here from Olympus on purpose to consult you. I was afraid you might be angry with me later on, if I went to the house of Okeanos without letting you know."

And Zeus said, "Hera, you can choose some other time for paying your visit to Okeanos - for the present let us devote ourselves to love

*and to the enjoyment of one another. Never yet have I been so overpow-
ered by passion neither for goddess nor mortal woman as I am at this
moment for yourself."*

*...Hera again answered him with a lying tale. "Most dread son of
Kronos," she exclaimed, "what are you talking about? Would you
have us enjoy one another here on the top of Mount Ida, where everything can be seen? What if one of the ever-living gods should see us
sleeping together, and tell the others? It would be such a scandal that
when I had risen from your embraces I could never show myself inside
your house again..." And Zeus answered, "Hera, you need not be
afraid that either god or man will see you, for I will enshroud both of us
in such a dense golden cloud, that the very sun for all his bright piercing
beams shall not see through it." With this the son of Kronos caught
his wife in his embrace. Whereon the earth sprouted them a cushion of
young grass, with dew-bespangled lotus, crocus, and hyacinth, so soft
and thick that it raised them well above the ground. Here they laid
themselves down and overhead they were covered by a fair cloud of gold,
from which there fell glittering dew-drops.*

*Thus, then, did the sire of all things repose peacefully on the crest
of Ida, overcome at once by sleep and love, and he held his spouse in
his arms.*

—tr. Samuel Butler, 1900

Anthesterion
February

The major festival this month is the Anthesteria, an early spring festival for Dionysus and Hermes Chthonios. The Attic town of Erchia also has a sacrifice to Dionysus early in the month. Anyone seeking initiation into the Greater Mysteries at Eleusis in the fall was supposed to be initiated into the Lesser Mysteries in Agrae this month first, so this is the first component of that cycle. Like the Mysteries in Boedromion, the Lesser Mysteries are a multi-day festival with many components. On the 23rd—overlapping with the Mysteries—Athens celebrated the Diasia for Zeus Meilichios, a chthonic, gentle version of the God who appears as snake. Take note of the following dates:

2nd of the month: a sacrifice to Dionysus in the Attic town of Erchia

11th–13th of the month: Anthesteria, a festival for Dionysus in Athens

20th–26th of the month: Lesser Mysteries in the town of Agrae in Attica

23rd of the month: Diasa, an Athenian festival for Zeus Meilichios

Anthesteria

When Dionysus was young, he stood by the edge of the sea. With his dark, flowing hair and robe of Tyrian purple, he looked like a prince. Pirates passing over the glimmering sea caught sight of him. Led on by the Fates, they mistook him for royalty and decided that he would make for a hefty ransom. Acting quickly, they jumped from their boat, and immediately dragged the God on board. They tried to tie his hands and feet but he was no prisoner and the ropes would not bind him—they simply fell away. As he sat unbound in their boat a smile came into his dark eyes and then the helmsman realized their impious act. He tried to convince his fellow sailors that they were trying to capture a son of Olympus, accusing them of madness for refusing to see that it was so. He did not know which God he was—Zeus or Apollon or Poseidon—but he urged them over and over to set the God free because he rightly feared the anger of the immortals.

The captain was not moved from his greed. Claiming the helmsman was out of his mind, he convinced the others that their captive was a prince likely spending his coins on a trip to Cyprus or Egypt, or even going to visit the far-off Hyperboreans of legend. Give him enough time, he said, and he will give us the names of his wealthy brothers who will ransom him. This, the captain claimed, was a great stroke of luck.

So they set sail. But soon there was an uncanny scent—overpoweringly sweet. Then wine flowed down all over the ship, streaming over the boards. The sailors were still staring in awe when ivy began to grow over the mast, in blossom and fruit at the same time. It twined upwards to the sail, where it met with a grapevine that was growing there, covering the whole cloth with the black fruit hanging down. They looked to the sides of the ship and saw that the tholepins were hung with garlands where oars should be.

The pirates begged the captain then to go back to land and release the captive, but it was too late for them. They heard a roar from the bow and turned to see that the God had taken the shape of a scowling lion. They turned again to see that now a bear was standing on its hind legs in the middle of the ship, ready to ravage them all. So the pirates ran back to where the helmsman was standing in the stern and they cowered there. The lion pounced on the captain and grasped him with claws and teeth. The terrified sailors jumped into the sea to keep from being devoured, and immediately were transformed into dolphins. Then the God turned to the helmsman and told him to be brave, that he held a favored place in the heart of loud-roaring Dionysus, the son of Semele and Zeus.

THE FESTIVAL

In the Anthesteria, the Athenians celebrate this grape-growing, life-bringing, awesome power of the God who came by ship. The name of the festival means "flowers", and it occurs just as the first flowers began to bloom, which is quite early in the mild Greek climate. In this festival, young children are garlanded with blossoms and were gifted with child sized, painted wine jars. In this guise, they represent a young Dionysus and remind all festival goers that he is the life-bringing God of all growing things. Arising from the association of the festival with childhood, this is the time of year when teachers would be paid. They hosted small gatherings for their students' families and received gifts from them.

There are three days to the festival and three distinct aspects. In addition to the focus on the growth of children and flowers, there is an emphasis on wine on the first day and second days and on placating the dead on the last. All things in the first parts of the Anthesteria are new—the wine is the new and is being tasted for the first time, the children and the flowers are young. The last part of the festival reminds worshippers of the limitations of life by focusing on placating spirits.

Day 1—Opening Jars. On the 11th of Anthesterion, the Athenians would open the *pithoi* fermenting jugs for the first sampling of the new wine. There was no racking process in which the wine was moved from the fermenting vessel to a cask or other secondary fermentation or aging vessel—the grape juice was simply sealed in the *pithos* and left untouched until this festival. The transformation must have seemed magical—as indeed it still does to the modern winemaker despite the relative complexity of the current process. Before the tasting began, some of the wine was carried to the sanctuary of Dionysus and placed on the altar as an offering. Then the new vintage would be mixed with water. Dionysus taught mankind the proper way to mix water and wine together and while wine was consumed in great quantity, it was diluted. The men would pray that the new wine would not harm them and would bring them blessings, and then the rest of the day was taken up with drinking, singing and dancing.

Day 2—Feast of the Wine Jars. The 12th was the main day of the festival. Named after the fat little jars in which wine was kept, miniature versions were given to children to carry in the parade to the altar of Dionysus. This procession included a float of a ship with a person dressed in costume and masked as Bakchos, a kind of sacred acting. He recalls the Homeric hymn in which a young Dionysus was captured by pirates. He turned himself into a lion on their ship and when the sailors leaped into the sea, he transformed them into dolphins. The festival procession was also a dramatic enactment of the God arriving at his temple as it was first opened because this particular shrine was only opened on this day. It was also a time when men would exchange ribald insults like women typically did at festivals of Demeter. There were also all the usual parts of a sacred procession: the girls who carried the barley baskets, men carrying all other items needed for sacrifice and of course, the goats to be sacrificed.

There were the sacrifices when they arrived at the temple and also secret rituals by the wife of the priest and fourteen other women—one for each of the altars to the God in his sanctuary. In sharp contrast to the wild abandon of the maenads, these women swore oaths testifying to their purity, temporary abstinence from sex and general fitness to perform religious rites. After the sacrifices were completed, there was a torch-led wedding procession to a separate building in a different part of the city. There the wife of the priest was married to Dionysus, just as the mortal Ariadne was after Theseus abandoned her on the island of Naxos. The wedding was consummated, so unless this was accomplished in some other way, someone—likely the priest—played the role of the God.

There was a darker side to this day. Other temples would close, Athenians would paint their doors black and the wine jars that gave their name to the day were then opened and the wine consumed in silence, by slaves as well as free Athenians. Citizens might attend a state banquet or celebrate the festival at home by inviting guests—who each brought their own wine—and drinking it silently. This was a remembrance of the tragic hero Orestes, who in myth arrived in Athens after being driven mad by murdering his mother to avenge his father. No one could speak to a person who had blood guilt staining his soul and so they drank for him in silence. Lest this seem too solemn, there was a prize of cakes or more wine for the first of the garlanded guests to drain their jars, which held about three quarts of watered wine. At the end of the feast, all the participants would place their garlands of flowers around their empty wine jars and dedicate them to the temple.

Day 3—Day of the Pots. The name of the 13th of Anthesterion comes from a cooking pot because worshippers would use it to make a dish of many seeds and vegetables cooked together. This symbolized the first meal after the mythical flood and was offered to Hermes Chthonios to pacify spirits. Hermes Chthonios is an ancient, phallic form of the messenger God who escorts the souls of the dead to the realm of Hades. The same face of the God marked boundaries in the form of pillars with faces and phalluses. The porridge was not consumed by the priests, and possibly also not by the worshippers because mortals did not usually share in offerings to an Underworld deity or to the spirits. There was also a procession of girls who carried water jars to a pit in a part of the Olympieion temple dedicated to Gaia. This was supposed to be the place where the flood began to drain away, and grain meal, honey and water were placed in it as offerings to the dead, particularly those who died in the flood.

In a return to the childlike playfulness of the first day of the Anthesteria, children would swing. Jars used during the festival were often decorated with images of garlanded children on swings. This was meant to soothe the souls of the dead and particularly to placate a ghost associated with a local Athenian tale. The story goes that Icarios was the first man to learn winemaking from Dionysus. When he gave wine to others, they mistook the unusual sensation of drunkenness to mean they'd been poisoned and so they killed him. His daughter Erigone hung herself in her grief. When her restless ghost caused a plague to devastate the city, the oracle of Delphi told the Athenians that her spirit could be appeased by hanging masks in the trees and having their children swing from them. While the children swinging on this day was playful and whimsical, it was also a magical act meant to ward off danger to the city.

When the Day of the Pots came to an end, worshippers would all shout to the spirits to go away because the Anthesteria are over.

Orphic Hymn to Liknitus[1] Bacchus
Liknitan Bacchus, bearer of the vine,
Thee I invoke to bless these rites divine.
Florid and gay, of nymphs the blossom bright,

---

1   Taylor translates "liknitus" as fan-bearer, but it might also refer to the basket of reeds the God was carried in as a baby.

And of fair Venus, Goddess of delight,
'Tis thine mad footsteps with mad
nymphs to beat,
Dancing through groves with lightly leaping feet.
From Jove's high counsels nursed by Proserpine,
And born the dread of all the powers divine:
Come, blessed power, regard thy
suppliant's voice,
Propitious come, and in these rites rejoice.

—tr. Thomas Taylor, 1792,
spelling modernized by M. Borden ·

Orphic Hymn to Terrestrial Hermes

Hermes I call, whom Fate decrees to dwell
In the dire path which leads to deepest hell.
O Bacchic Hermes, progeny divine
Of Dionysius, parent of the vine,
And of celestial Venus Paphian queen…
…To wretched souls the leader of the way
When Fate decrees, to regions void of day.
Thine is the wand which causes sleep to fly,
Or lulls to slumberous rest the weary eye.
For Proserpine through Tartarus dark and wide
Gave thee forever flowing souls to guide.
Come, blessed power the sacrifice attend,
And grant our mystic works a happy end.

—tr. Thomas Taylor, 1792,
spelling modernized by M. Borden

The Lesser Mysteries

The mystai at the Greater Mysteries at Eleusis in the Fall were supposed to have been initiated into the Lesser Mysteries at Agrae in the Spring. According to the legend, Herakles was the first initiate into the Lesser Mysteries. He had wanted to be initiated at Eleusis but as a foreigner to Attica, at that time initiation was closed to him. The rites of the Lesser Mysteries were created for his benefit. They remain a secret but they

Herakles and Athena

probably included a focus on purification. There are images of Heracles with Kore and Demeter, washing himself to be purified of blood guilt and ritual bathing is one of the only known aspect of the rites.

Orphic Hymn to Hercules

Hear, powerful Hercules untamed and strong,
To whom vast hands, and mighty works
belong…
…Magnanimous, in divination skilled
And in the athletic labours of the field.
'Tis thine strong archer, all things to devour,
Supreme, all-helping, all-producing power…
…Unwearied, earth's best blossom, offspring fair,
To whom calm peace, and peaceful works are
dear….
… Supremely skilled, thou reignest in heaven's
abodes,
Thyself a God amidst the immortal Gods.
With arms unshaken, infinite, divine,
Come, blessed power, and to our rites incline;
The mitigations of disease convey,
And drive disastrous maladies away.
Come, shake the branch with thy almighty arm,
Dismiss thy darts and noxious fate disarm.

—tr. Thomas Taylor, 1792,
spelling modernized by M. Borden

Diasia

The Diasia festival honored Zeus Meilichios, an ancient form of Zeus whose name means "friendly," or "kind." He was an Underworld deity with the shape of a snake, and the title could be a euphemism like "the kindly ones" for the Furies. In late periods the snake began to show up in depictions of Olympian Zeus, but the purely chthonic form is older. He is shown in areas outside Athens as a seated older man, and was also a God worshipped in the household, so there may have been an ancestral aspect to his cult. He is also shown with a cornucopia, so he is connected to the fertility of the soil and the agricultural cycle.

His ancestral associations are what tie the chthonic Zeus Meilichios to the heavenly Zeus, who is the father of Gods and men. His immense power, his fecundity, the potency of his protection—all evoke the dominion of fatherhood. While the awe-inspiring might of heavenly Zeus—the authoritative God in the public sphere—can be overwhelming, Meilichios is the gentler, more accessible father who is known primarily at home, and whose interest as an ancestor lies with protecting the family, promoting its prosperity and ensuring its survival. This milder Zeus gently guides for the betterment of the clan.

Zeus Meilichios was honored by priests in Winter at the Pompaia, but the Diasa was a festival for the people. There were feasts and children received gifts. Offerings at the Diasia were given by each household and could be bloodless—animal-shaped cakes, grain and fruit. However, Zeus Meilichios received animal sacrifices at other times and it is possible that the ram's wool used in the Pompaia was from an animal slain at the Diasia. All these offerings were given to the God completely, as humans did not share in the food given to the Gods and Spirits beneath the Earth.

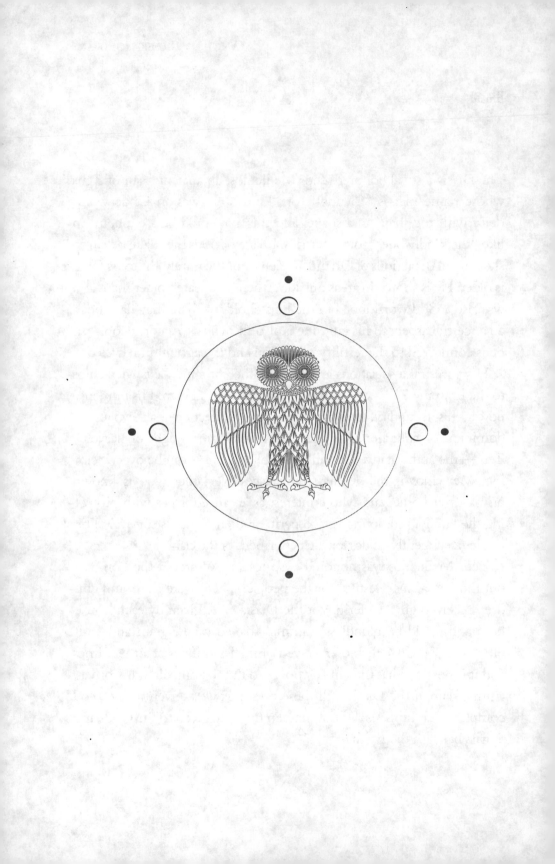

Elaphebolion
March

There is little known about the festival that gave this month its name. The most significant festival this month is the City Dionysia, an Athenian festival for Dionysus. The last day of the Dionysia is called the Pandia, and it consists of a mock investigation into all the disorderly conduct of the festival. The festival for Asclepius the day before the Dionysia begins is also a significant holiday. Individuals made sacrifices to Kronos on the 15th, but this was a private, household observance rather than a state celebration. Take note of the following dates:

6th of the month: Elaphebolia, an Athenian festival for Artemis the Huntress

9th of the month: Asclepieia, an Athenian festival for Asclepius

10th–17th of the month: City Dionysia, a festival for Dionysus

15th of the month: private sacrifices to Kronos in Athens

17th of the month: Pandia, an investigation following the City Dionysia

Elaphebolia

Elaphebolia is a title of Artemis meaning "deer-shooter," one of the primary epithets of the Goddess. This festival should be honored on the 6th, as that is her day every month. Although few specifics are known, other cities celebrated this festival as well and the appropriate sacrifice was a deer or cakes shaped like deer.

Homeric Hymn 27 to Artemis

I sing of Artemis, whose shafts are of gold, who cheers on the hounds, the pure maiden, shooter of stags, who delights in archery, own sister to Apollo with the golden sword.

Over the shadowy hills and windy peaks she draws her golden bow, rejoicing in the chase, and sends out grievous shafts. The tops of the high mountains tremble and the tangled wood echoes awesomely with the outcry of beasts. Earth quakes and the sea also where fishes shoal. But the goddess with a bold heart turns every way destroying the race of wild beasts.

And when she is satisfied and has cheered her heart, this huntress who delights in arrows slackens her supple bow and goes to the great house of her dear brother Phoebus Apollo, to the rich land of Delphi, there to order the lovely dance of the Muses and Graces. There she hangs up her curved bow and her arrows, and heads and leads the dances, gracefully arrayed, while all they utter their heavenly voice, singing how neat-ankled Leto bare children supreme among the immortals both in thought and in deed.

Hail to you, children of Zeus and rich-haired Leto! And now I will remember you and another song also.

—tr. Hugh Evelyn–White, 1914

Asclepieia

Apollon loved Coronis, a princess of Thessaly. She was unfaithful to him, a truth Apollon did not wish to hear. Ravens were still white at that time, but when one of those winged gossipers whispered the truth in the ear of the God, Apollon in his rage made that bird and all its descendants black forever. He killed Coronis even though she was pregnant with his child, and snatched the baby right off the faithless girl's funeral pyre.

He carried the infant Asclepius to the wise centaur Chiron, who raised him to have great skill and wisdom. He taught him to hunt and also to heal. As he grew, Asclepius became the best physician and surgeon the land had ever known. Athena herself gifted him with the blood of the Gorgon, which he used to devise cunning new medicines. The blood from the veins on the left side of the Gorgon's body could cause illness and death, but with the blood from the right side he could heal any patient, even one beyond death. And so the healing God—still a man, then—began to raise the dead, to the rejoicing of humankind. This irked the eternal Gods because Asclepius was cheating Hades of his subjects and upending the order of all things. Zeus struck him down with a lightning bolt.

Unable to hurt his great father, Apollon struck back at the Cyclopes who made the bolt, killing them. In return, Zeus humbled him, forcing Apollon to live on Earth for a time as a servant to a cowherd. That year, every one of those cows had twins. Zeus placed the body of Asclepius in the stars, where he stood holding up snakes for all to see. After Apollon's year of service was up, he interceded with his father, and so Zeus brought Asclepius to Olympus and gave him a seat among the immortals.

In the temple of Asclepius at Epidauros—where the walls were covered in prayers to the God and inscriptions from those he'd healed detailing their miraculous recoveries—pilgrims in search of healing would come to consult with the priests, sometimes waiting for weeks or months for an appointment. After making sacrifices and undergoing purifications, the suppliants would incubate a dream by sleeping in the temple. They would dream that the God himself healed them or sometimes that one of the snakes that lived in the temple grounds had come to intercede in some way, such as licking a festering wound that upon waking would be discovered to have closed itself. Asclepius' sanctuary was full of votive offerings—thousands of little clay body parts representing what he had healed—as well as the dogs and serpents that roamed freely.

The cult of Asclepius was introduced to Athens in the classical period, and the playwright Sophocles had a role in arranging the location of his temple, which was near the Dionysiac Theater. Roosters were common sacrifices there and Socrates' last words after drinking his hemlock were that he owed one to the healing God. Few details survive about the Athenian festival for Asclepius on the 9th of Elaphebolion—only that the sacrifice was large. Common meals were part of his worship in other regions, so there was probably a feast in addition to consuming the meat of the sacrificed animals.

Orphic Hymn to Asclepius

Great Asclepius, skilled to heal mankind,
All-ruling Pæan, and physician kind...
Strong lenient God, regard my suppliant prayer,
Bring gentle Health,[1] adorned with lovely hair.
Convey the means of mitigating pain,

---

1   Hygeia was the personification of health. She is named in this hymn as the wife of Asclepius but was more commonly considered to be his daughter or sister.

And raging, deadly pestilence restrain.
O power all–flourishing, abundant, bright,
Apollo's honored offspring, God of light,
Husband of blameless Health, the constant foe
Of dread Disease the minister of woe.
Come, blessed saviour, and my health defend,
And to my life afford a prosperous end.

–tr. Thomas Taylor, 1792,
spelling modernized by M. Borden

Asclepius and Telesphorus

City Dionysia

There were festivals for Dionysus in many parts of Greece and these all shared a sense of normal social order being suspended. There are many myths in various regions in Greece about Dionysus initially being rejected by the populace and having to force his cult to be instituted. In Athens, the story went that when Dionysus first arrived there after his birth, he was not welcomed or given due worship. He punished the city by striking all the men with a venereal disease. They consulted the oracle, which told them to institute the worship of Dionysus with phallic processions.

The form of the God worshipped at this festival was Dionysus Eleuthereus, from the town of Eleutherai on the border of Attica. The cult statue moved to Athens in an early period was originally a column, which was common in the bronze age. Sometime during the archaic period, a terracotta mask with a beard was added to the column. Dionysus Eleuthereus had a temple on the south slope of the Acropolis near the spot where the Dionysian theater eventually was constructed. Before the holiday, the wooden cult statue was removed to the grove of the Academy. Once the festival began with dithyrambic choruses, the statue was carried to the temple in the phallic procession ordained by the oracle.

The parade had non-citizens in purple robes bearing trays of bread and other offerings, citizens carrying wineskins on their shoulders and a maiden chosen from the upper classes carrying a golden basket of fruit and grapes. Bulls and goats were driven and dragged along. There were giant phalluses constructed from wood, not just from Athens but also sent by all the cities owing tribute to Athens. These were carried to the temple with the statue and offerings. There were satyrs—men dressed in costumes that included animal ears, masks, animal skins, horses' tails and oversized erect phalluses.

The procession paused at shrines along the way to perform dances before the altars of various Gods. Once it arrived at the altar in front of the temple, the victims were slaughtered—hundreds of goats and bulls. Afterwards, there was a revel known for its licentiousness. This lasted through the night, with men carrying torches through the streets with music, song and dance.

It is likely from these informal choruses of men singing and dancing in the revels that dramas originated. While their precise origins are unclear, theatric performances certainly came from the cult of Dionysus and the word "tragedy" is related to *tragos* (goat)—the primary sacrifice to the God who gave theater to humankind.

What set the Dionysia in the city of Athens apart from similar festivals in other regions was the element of public dramatic performance. The theatric competition at this festival was the most prestigious poetic competition in Greece. The judges were very difficult to bribe because their names were drawn out of jars at the beginning of the festival. There were ten judges and each listed the names of the poets in order of quality once all performances had been completed, and placed these lists in another jar. The archon drew five lists out of the jar and the majority between those five won the competition. To bribe all potential judges or even just the final ten would be extremely costly and logistically challenging. The prizes for the winning poets were bulls and goats, which were then expected to be sacrificed to the God.

The masks worn by actors on the ancient Greek stage recall the cult masks from the original column. While cult masks may have also been worn, the actors' masks covered the entire head while the masks of the God covered only the face.

There were four days of performances which lasted all day. The audience would watch three tragedies back to back in the morning. These were followed by a satyr play, a performance of bawdy humor in which the chorus were dressed as satyrs. After an afternoon break—this time of year is lovely weather in Greece for watching outdoor performances but the afternoon Sun can still be intense—there would be a comedy in the evening.

The Dionysiac Theater was built to accommodate the festival performances of the Dionysia. It could hold seventeen thousand spectators in its audience, meaning that announcements before plays became binding public pronouncements. For example, you could free a slave by having it announced in this way—making the prior owner appear both wealthy and magnanimous.

The core aspects of the festival were the phallic procession, the revel and the theatrical performances. All three presented opportunities to express and release both positive and negative emotions—a purifying catharsis.

From *The Frogs* by Aristophanes

Iacchus,[1] venerated god, hasten at our call.
Iacchus, oh! Iacchus! Come into this meadow,
thy favourite resting-place.
Come to direct the sacred choirs of the Initiate.
May a thick crown of fruit-laden myrtle
branches rest on thy head
and may thy bold foot step this free and
joyful dance,
taught us by the Graces—this pure, religious
measure,
that our sacred choirs rehearse.

—tr. The Athenian Society (likely Oscar Wilde ,) 1912

---

1   Iacchus is another transliteration of *Iakchos*—a name for Dionysus used in the Eleusinian Mysteries.

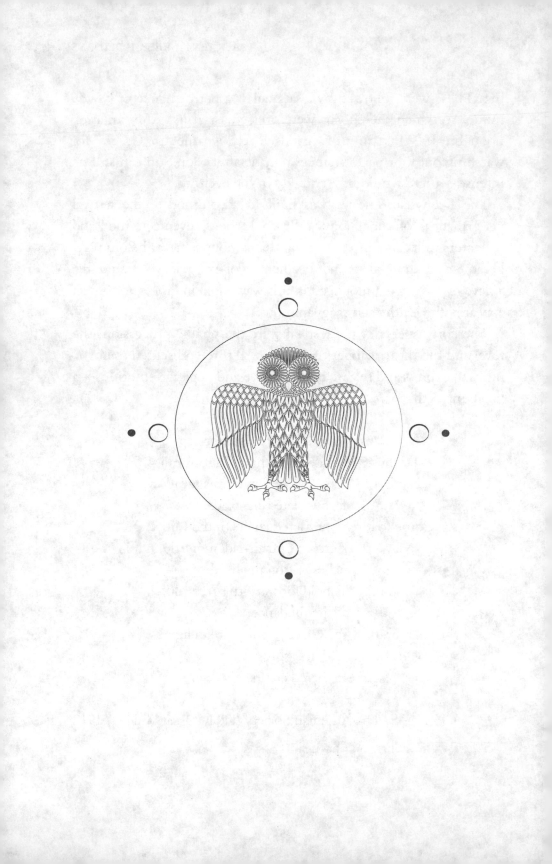

Munichion
April

With Spring well underway, there are several minor festivals this month. On the 4th the Athenians celebrated the festival of Eros and the 19th of the month sees a military parade for Olympian Zeus. Two festivals between these are dedicated to Artemis—the Munichia and the procession to the Delphinion, the temple of Apollon which served as a court for murder trials. If it seems odd that the temple is his while the procession is hers, remember that the divine twins often share and each shows up regularly in the stories of the other. Artemis was venerated in the Delphinion as well.

There are two sacrifices later in the month by Erchia, a town in Attica. The first is to Leucaspis, a prince killed by Herakles. This would have been a chthonic sacrifice into the ground rather than one at a raised altar as he was a dead hero and not a God, and the people would not have shared in the offerings. The second sacrifice is to the Tritopatores. These were the ancestors of the community or tribe as a whole rather than of individuals, and various towns across Greece venerated their forebears under this title. The Athenians included both prayers and sacrifices to them in their marriage rites, so they had an interest in the clan carrying on and in its ongoing fertility and prosperity. The followers of Orpheus associated them with the winds. As with Leucaspis, sacrifices to the Tritopatores would have been chthonic offerings. Take note of the following dates:

4th of the month: Festival of Eros in Athens

6th of the month: Procession for Artemis to the Delphinion in Athens

16th of the month: Munichia, an Athenian festival for Artemis

19th of the month: Olympieia in Athens

20th of the month: sacrifice to Leucaspis in the Attic town of Erchia

21st of the month: sacrifice to the Tritopatores in the Attic town of Erchia

Festival of Eros

No specifics of the festival of Eros on the 4th of Munichion survive, other than that there was a festival. Eros himself is the personification of desire, and particularly of homoerotic desire. He took the form of a young man and represented the Greek ideal of masculine beauty—athletic yet boyish. Plato says that humankind completely misunderstood the exceptional importance of Eros and goes on to describe three genders. Masculinity, he said, came from the Sun, femininity from the Earth and the third gender from the Moon. This last included both male and female characteristics, had an androgynous aesthetic and was powerfully strong. Its might was so great that the Gods themselves were threatened and Zeus ordered Apollon to cut every human into two. This splitting caused longing for the other half of the soul, creating both desire and sex. Some sex was for children, and some for pleasure, the uniting of self with self. Lesbians arose from this splitting and desire for reunion, as they were halves of the original feminine gender that came completely from the Earth. Sex between men in particular gave men both satisfaction and desire to pursue greatness outside the home. These were the manliest of men, the best suited for politics. Their desire was spiritual as well as physical, encompassing their whole being.

Desire is truly the longing for wholeness, and the happiness of all humankind lies in love. Eros is the love not just of the human other, but of all things good and beautiful. As wisdom is beautiful, Eros leads to wisdom. And as desire can produce children, it leads to immortality as well, through human children and through the offspring of the mind, an even more lasting glory. All the genders of love produce immortality, because Eros is first a physical desire, then an aesthetic one and last an intellectual and spiritual one that leaves the soul in awe of the universe and eternal beauty.

It is this last form of Eros that Hesiod frames as the original creative force of the world. Out of the primordial chaos came Earth and Eros, Darkness and Night. From desire, Earth bore the Sky and from their union came all the Gods and the world.

The winged God of love, Eros

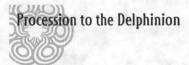

Procession to the Delphinion

When Apollon had taken the valley at Delphi from the Python, he laid the foundations of his shrine. He needed priests for his new temple who could guide worshippers in making proper sacrifice. Looking out to the wine-dark sea the one who works from afar saw a Cretan ship. These sailors from Knossos were trading in the area, and Phoebus decided to meet them. He took the form of a dolphin and leapt up onto the deck of their ship. The sailors tried to pitch the creature back into the sea but it was so large that the swaying effort made the shipboards creak and groan. So they sailed on, with the dolphin still watching them from the deck. They did not understand, but they could see that its eyes remained on them and tracked their movements. So the sailors decided to put into a port, thinking perhaps the dolphin would leap back into the sea on its own when it saw that they were leaving the ship. But the ship would not steer and it traced the coast all along the peninsula of the Peloponnese—Apollon was guiding the sails with the wind. They sailed all along the South of Greece and came up the west side of the country until Zeus blew them to go back eastward again, leading them to harbor.

As the ship came onto the sand, Apollon jumped down from it, flashing with fire and shining so brightly he seemed like a star in the noonday sun. He entered his own shrine and the tripods lit up with flames, filling the temple with radiance. Then he returned to the ship, appearing to the sailors like a young man. He played the part, greeting them as if he did not know who they were or why they had come. They asked him where they were and told them that one of the Gods had guided their ship to land there.

Engraving of Apollon attended by Nymphs

Apollon revealed himself to them and gave them his name. He told them his plan for them, that they would be the priests of his temple and deliver oracles to guide all humankind. He taught them to sing "Ie Paean" and they made an offering of barley there on the beach, on an altar called Delphinius because the God had taken the shape of the dolphin. And so the far shooter claimed another name and he is called Delphinius as well. The sailors poured a libation to the blessed Gods and then feasted there in the sand. Apollon himself led them up to the temple, playing the lyre as they climbed, singing "Ie Paean" the whole way. The God showed them his temple and assured them that their days of toil and labor were over. If they served him there, no matter how many throats of sheep they cut, they would never run out of meat and they would never know hunger. But if they were faithless to him, they would always work and be subject to cruel masters.

Apollon had a temple in Athens under his name Delphinius and when the maidens of Athens processed to the Delphinion they walked as suppliants, carrying olive branches wrapped in wool. This was in part a commemoration—the hero-king Theseus offered just such a bough to Apollo on the day he sailed for Crete, which was the 6th of Munichion. The girls of Athens also supplicated Artemis on the 6th, which was her day in every month.

The divine Huntress was the queen of all wild places, and Homer calls her *Potnia Theron*, the Mistress of Animals. As a young girl, she made her father Zeus swear to never make her marry, and so she is a Goddess always of female selfhood and self-rule. Any man who comes upon her unawares and violates the sanctity of her chastity—even with his eyes—she mercilessly strikes down. She wears the short dress and hairstyle of a young girl, free to run with her hunting hounds, carrying her bow. She can be glimpsed running through the woods, chasing deer and dancing with her nymph companions. Young women danced at her festivals as the nymphs danced around her in the woods, and likely did so in the procession to the Delphinion. Artemis is protector of girls and releases them when they are married—an offering to her is part of the marriage rite. She continues to watch over them in childbirth, a service for which she occasionally took her own sacrifice—women who died in the process were struck down by Artemis and their clothes were dedicated to her shrine.

Homeric Hymn 9 to Artemis

Muse, sing of Artemis, sister of the Far-shooter, the virgin who delights in arrows, who was fostered with Apollo. She waters her horses from Meles deep in reeds, and swiftly drives her all-golden chariot through Smyrna to vine-clad Claros where Apollo, god of the silver bow, sits waiting for the far-shooting goddess who delights in arrows.

–tr. Hugh Evelyn-White, 1912

Munichia

In the procession of the Munichia, girls between the ages of five and ten dressed in yellow robes and acted like bears. The ritual of girls imitating bears in her procession was a rite of atonement: there was a legend that a bear sacred to the Goddess was killed in her shrine by the young men of Attica. In her rage, Artemis tormented all of Athens with a plague. An oracle revealed that the only way to assuage the Goddess was for someone to sacrifice a daughter to her. At first no father was willing to part with his beloved child, but seeing the suffering of all, a man called Embaros finally came forward. He approached the altar with his daughter but at the last minute hid her in the sanctuary and cut the throat of a female goat dressed up in the girl's clothing instead. In gratitude for saving the city, the family of Embaros was appointed to the priesthood of Artemis for the remainder of their lives. Demanding the sacrifice of a daughter was not an uncommon request by Artemis in literature and was usually followed by a switch with an animal.

Artemis herself was envisioned in the form of a bear in the Attic city of Brauron, and Artemis Brauronia had a sanctuary on the Acropolis in Athens. The practice of girls acting like bears comes from the Brauronia cult, as well as the story of bear slaying in the temple. Athenian girls were required to spend time serving the Goddess at Brauron dressed as bears. Before they became women, girls had at least four special roles in religious rites, including carrying sacred objects by night underground to a sanctuary of Aphrodite, grinding grain to make offering cakes for Athena, acting the bear for Artemis and carrying baskets in procession.

A special offering was also carried in Mounichia procession—a cake with lit candles arranged in a circle, reminiscent of the moonlight. If the month began on the New Moon, the Full Moon was typically celebrated on the 16th, so this holiday has a clear lunar aspect. These shining cakes were offered to the Artemis at other times of year as well as a sacrifice by individuals.

From *Hippolytus* by Euripedes

All hail! Most beauteous Artemis, lovelier far
than all the daughters of Olympus!
For thee, O mistress mine, I bring this woven
wreath, culled from a virgin meadow,
where nor shepherd dares to herd his flock nor
ever scythe hath mown,
but o'er the mead unshorn the bee doth wing its
way in spring,
and with the dew from rivers drawn purity that
garden tends.
Such as know no cunning lore, yet in whose
nature self-control, made perfect, hath a home,
these may pluck the flowers, but not the
wicked world.
Accept, I pray, dear mistress, mine this chaplet
from my holy hand to crown thy locks of gold.

—tr. E.P. Colerige, 1910

Olympieia

The Olympieia on the 19th of Munichion was a military display—including a procession of cavalry—in honor of Olympian Zeus. Unrelated to the Olympic games, there were various mounted exercises in the hippodrome with mock pursuits at constantly increasing speeds. Their purpose was practical as well as celebratory. The complicated formations of the Olympieia were important operations on the battlefield. To prepare for the festival, a soldier was also preparing for war. Athens first celebrated this holiday in the 6th century BCE when work began on the temple of Olympian Zeus. An Ionic temple that was likely imitating the magnificent temples of Ephesus, Miletus and the islands, it was considerably larger than the Doric temples or older archaic shrines of Athens. The sacrifice at this festival was equally colossal. Hecatombs of bulls were offered to Zeus, so the feast would be magnificent.

The annual festival commemorated the date the ground was struck for the foundations, but construction on the temple itself continued for nearly 700 years and was completed by the Roman emperor Hadrian. He also augmented the festival itself by adding *agones*—athletic contests. He built many monuments in Athens including a library, a pantheon, an aqueduct, a triumphal arch and a bridge. The modern Àdrianou Street that bears his name has many charming shops and restaurants along its route that still winds through Athens on the same path as it did thousands of years ago.

from Orphic Hymn to Zeus

Our prayers and expiations, king divine,
For all things round thy head exalted shine.
The earth is thine, and mountains swelling high,

The sea profound, and all within the sky.
Saturnian king, descending from above,
Magnanimous, commanding, sceptered Jove,
All-parent, principle and end of all,
Whose power almighty, shakes this earthly ball.
Even Nature trembles at thy mighty nod,
Loud-sounding, armed with lightning,
thundering God.
Source of abundance, purifying king,
O various-formed from whom all natures spring.
Propitious hear my prayer, give blameless health,
With peace divine, and necessary wealth.

−tr. Thomas Taylor, 1792,
spelling modernized by M. Borden

Zeus with an eagle

Thargelion
May

This month is named after the Thargelia festival of Apollon. Activities on both the 6th (the day of Artemis) and the 7th (the day of Apollon) are associated with this holiday. Thargelion sees the rare holiday celebrated in Athens that is dedicated to a foreign deity—the Bendidia for Bendis, a Thracian Goddess of hunting and the Moon. At the end of the month, there are two rites for Athena focused on the upkeep of the temple and cult statue. These would make an excellent occasion to clean and refresh any personal or household shrines.

There are three Erchian sacrifices this month. The first is to Pythian Apollon, along with his parents Leto and Zeus, the messenger God Hermes and the Dioskouroi. These were the twin princes of Sparta, Castor and Polydeuces—one mortal and one divine, both mounted on horseback. Conceived on the same night, Castor was the son of Leda and the Spartan king Tyndarius, while his twin brother Polydeuces was fathered by Zeus in the form of a swan. Their hero cult was widespread in Sparta as well as other regions of Greece and the twins were seen as saviors of those in trouble, particularly at sea. The second Erchian sacrifice is to Zeus Epacrios—Zeus of the Mountains Heights, associated with the mountain ranges of Attica and their snows. The last sacrifice is to Menedeius, a hero local to Erchia. Take note of the following dates:

4th of the month: sacrifice to Leto, Pythian Apollon, Zeus, Hermes and the Dioskouroi in the Attic town of Erchia

6th–7th of the month: Thargelia, an Athenian festival for Apollon

16th of the month: sacrifice to Zeus Epacrios in the Attic town of Erchia

19th of the month: Bendidia, an Athenian festival for the Thracian Goddess Bendis

19th of the month: sacrifice to the Menedeius in the Attic town of Erchia

24th of the month: Kallynteria, an Athenian rite for Athena

25th of the month: Plynteria, an Athenian rite for Athena

Homeric Hymn to the Dioskouroi

Bright-eyed Muses, tell of the Tyndaridae, the Sons of Zeus, glorious children of neat-ankled Leda, Castor the tamer of horses, and blameless Polydeuces. When Leda had lain with the dark-clouded Son of Cronos, she bare them beneath the peak of the great hill Taygetus, children who are deliverers of men on earth and of swift-going ships when stormy gales rage over the ruthless sea. Then the shipmen call upon the sons of great Zeus with vows of white lambs, going to the forepart of the prow; but the strong wind and the waves of the sea lay the ship under water, until suddenly these two are seen darting through the air on tawny wings. Forthwith they allay the blasts of the cruel winds and still the waves upon the surface of the white sea: fair signs are they and deliverance from toil. And when the shipmen see them they are glad and have rest from their pain and labour.

Hail, Tyndaridae, riders upon swift horses!

—tr. Hugh Evelyn–White, 1914

Thargelia

Boundaries were essential to the ancient Greek mind. They marked the lines between the sacred precinct of a God and the profane world, between domestic and foreign, the city and the countryside, the home and the public sphere and there were steles and images Gods to mark them and protect the liminal spaces between. Purification did not eradicate evil as much as it removed it beyond the boundary of the self, just as water doesn't cause dirt to disappear but carries it elsewhere, leaving the bather clean. Typical purificatory rites involved both water—especially running water—and blood. Before the Mysteries at Eleusis, the mystai bathe in the sea and are sprinkled with the blood of the sacrificed piglets. In the *Iliad*, to end the plague, even after the Greek soldiers returned the daughter of Apollon's priest, they had to wash themselves, throw the water into the sea and then sacrifice to the God. Apollon in particular was associated with purification and Apollon himself cleansed Orestes of his blood guilt by sacrificing a pig over him so that he would be washed in its blood.

The Thargelia festival was primarily a purificatory rite of Apollon with the purpose of protecting the coming harvest and washing it of any evil that might be brought into the city. Like in other purification rites, the second part was sacrifice, but the first was a different practice than the typical bathing, although similar rites were carried out in other Greek cities. From among the poor and the ugly of the city, the Athenians chose two *pharmakoi*—scapegoats. They lived richly for a while, eating barley, cheese and figs at the expense of the city. When the 6th of Thargelion arrived, the Athenians offered a ram to Demeter Chloe—Demeter of Blooming Plants, and then the pharmakoi donned necklaces of figs. The pharmakos representing the men of Athens wore black figs and the one representing the women wore white figs. They were processed all around the city. The citizens beat them with fig branches and threw plants at them, and drove them out of the city, across its boundaries. This was probably a softer adaptation of an earlier version of the ritual in which the pharmakoi were beaten with sticks and stoned. There is an important element of contagion in the rite—what doesn't touch you can't clean you. By eating the city's food and being paraded all around it, the pharmakoi with their close contact absorb all the evil of the community and then are driven across the boundary just like the wash water is thrown into the sea.

Just as other forms of purification require immediate sacrifice to the Gods afterwards, the 7th of Thargelion was the day of sacrifices. There was a procession, and bulls and goats bled out on the altar alongside a special offering to Apollon—all the early vegetables cooked together, a first fruits offering to ensure the coming harvest. The Pyanepsia had a similar offering of grains, beans and vegetables. In both these festivals, Apollon takes on aspects of a deity of vegetation—an impure harvest cannot be a good harvest and Apollon is the purifier.

This day was also important to the phratrai—the religious societies claiming a common ancestor. Apollon was the Phratros, the father of an ancestor of all the Athenians, and in this capacity he was also a protector of boys as Artemis was of girls. The phratrai organized a singing competition of choruses of 50 singers each. There were five choruses of men and five choruses of boys and the prize was a tripod that would be dedicated to Apollon in his shrine called the Pythion.

Bendidia

The Goddess Bendis came to Athens from Thrace, a region directly northeast of the Aegean Sea, covering parts of modern Turkey Bulgaria, and Greece. Her worship was established in the fifth century BCE as part of a political alliance. The oracle of Zeus at Dodona—where the voice of the God could be heard in the rustling leaves of the oak grove—sanctioned its import. She was a huntress and Goddess of the Moon, and was shown wearing a short dress with a hunting spear. Despite these similarities, Bendis was her own Goddess and was not venerated as a form of Artemis.

Offering to Artemis Bendis

Polytheism is dynamic—far from being a set of rigid beliefs and inert practices, it is a living thing in constant flux, vibrant and mutable in both practice and theology. Within Greece, the pantheon was not static and changed over time. Some Gods of the classical era are attested in Mycenaean Linear B tablets of a thousand years prior—and some are not, meaning they were introduced in the intervening years. Likewise, some of the Mycenaean God names disappear, whether the divinities themselves changed names or were forgotten. Greek polytheists never assumed their own Gods to be the only ones in the world, either. When they encountered the Gods of other cultures, sometimes they assumed them to be the same as their own Gods. The names might be different, but the God would be the same, because a name is just a word and as an apple is an apple regardless of the words in any given language, so with the Gods. At other times, though, they did not syncretize their deities with those of foreign religions, even when it would seem intuitive. Bendis in many ways appears to be extremely similar to Artemis, but the Athenians venerated her under her own name instead of identifying her with their local Goddess.

The Bendidia festival was celebrated with a procession from Athens to Piraeus, the city's port where Bendis had a shrine. The worshippers would wash after they arrived, and then would eat. As dusk fell, they began to prepare for the main contest, which was a torch relay race on horseback. The celebrations afterwards lasted through the night.

Kallynteria and Plynteria

Late in the month are two festival occasions which centered on the cleaning and upkeep of the temple and statue of Athena, the Kallynteria and the Plynteria. There are few details about the Kallynteria, but the name suggests sweeping. This would have been a time to clean the temple and perhaps also to maintain the lamp that was kept always burning there and to refill it with olive oil. The massive gold lamp was supposed to hold enough oil to burn for a year, but the fuel had to be replenished eventually.

The Plynteria was the day on which the cult statue of Athena was washed. This was done by the Praxiergidai family who had this duty as a special, inherited privilege. They treated it as a clandestine rite and executed their duties with solemnity. The original statue was wooden and was carried to the sea to be cleansed there because running water was more purifying than still water. Attica is an arid region and there are few streams that would be able to accommodate this function in this hotter time of year, and the sea was also especially purifying. Other shrines all closed for the occasion and this was considered a generally unlucky day in Athens, so no business was conducted. Perhaps this was because the image of the Goddess had to leave her temple or because the dross that was cleansed from her also belonged to the city or represented a kind of drifting evil.

There is a story from Argos that Athena had a favorite attendant among the women of Thebes. She was the mother of Tiresias, who would become the great seer of myth. One day as the Goddess and her mortal companion bathed together in a spring, the boy Tiresias wandered the area with his hunting dogs. It was near midday and the unbearded youth, hot from the sun and the chase, was driven by thirst to the water where his mother and Athena waded, exposed. He chanced to catch sight of the unclothed maiden Goddess and was immediately struck blind, noon turned to midnight behind his eyes. His mother raged, laying this awful fate at the feet of the Goddess. But Athena told her that it is the law of Zeus, the son of Cronus, that terrible punishment awaits any person who lays eyes on any of the immortal Gods without their knowledge and consent. And she gave Tiresias a greater sight and his gift of prophecy brought him great renown, so that thousands of years after his death, his name still lingers on the lips of any who would know the future. Perhaps this belief lingered in the taboos of the Plynteria, lest some chance glimpse bring suffering to Athens.

Before the statue could be transported, the women of the Praxiergidai undressed it and removed all jewelry and other ornaments. Then they wrapped it in cloth and carried it to the water in a sacred procession led by a woman bearing a basket of fig cakes. This was not a public event, or a festive procession, as no one was allowed to see the Goddess unclothed. Once at the sea, the women unwrapped the statue and two who were specially appointed to the task would wash it in the waves. The peplos may have been washed at the same time. Then the Goddess was rewrapped for the return journey. The Acropolis is about five miles from the sea, so this process took much of the day. The procession returned by torchlight. In the freshly washed temple the statue would then be unwrapped a final time, redressed in the peplos and would have had its jewelry and golden crown placed back on. You can imagine how, in the flickering light, with her ornament restored to her, the plain wooden idol would seem to come to life.

Excerpts from Callimachus Hymn 5, On the Bath of Pallas

All ye that are companions of the Bath of Pallas, come forth, come forth! I heard but now the snorting of the sacred steeds, and the goddess is ready to go. Haste ye now, O fair-haired daughters of Pelasgus, haste! Never did Athena wash her mighty arms before she drave the dust from the flanks of her horses—not even when, her armour all defiled with filth, she returned from the battle of the lawless Giants, but first she loosed from the care her horses' necks, and in the springs of Oceanus washed the flecks of sweat and from their mouths that champed the bit cleansed the clotted foam.

Come forth, Athena! A company pleasing to thy heart awaits thee, the maiden daughters of Acestor's mighty sons…Come forth, Athena, Sacker of Cities, golden-helmeted, who rejoicest in the din of horse and shield. Today, ye water-carriers, dip not your pitchers—today, O Argos, drink ye from the fountains and not from the river. Today, ye handmaid-ens carry your pitchers to Physadeia, or Amymone,[1] daughter of Danaus. For, mingling his waters with gold and with flowers, Inakhos will come from his pastoral hills, bringing fair water for the Bath of Athena. But beware, O Pelasgian, lest even unwittingly thou behold the Queen. Whoso shall behold Pallas, Keeper of Cities, naked, shall look on Argos for this the last time.

Maidens, one nymph of old in Thebes did Athena love much, yea beyond all her companions, even the mother of Teiresias, and was never apart from her. Yet even her did many tears await in the after days, albeit she was a comrade pleasing to the heart of Athena. One day those twain undid the buckles of their robes beside the fair-flowing Fountain of the Horse on Helicon and bathed, and noontide quiet held all the hill. Those two ere bathing and it was the noontide hour and a great quiet held that hill. Only Teiresias, on whose cheek the down was just darkening, still ranged with his hounds the holy place. And, athirst beyond telling, he came unto the flowing fountain, wretched man! And unwillingly saw that which is not lawful to be seen. [Athena] spake and night seized the eyes of the youth. And he stood there speechless; for pain glued his knees

---

1 Physadeia and Amymone are springs and Inakhos is a river God

and helplessness stayed his voice. But the nymph cried: "What has thou done to my boy, lady? Is such the friendship of you goddesses? Thou hast taken away the eyes of my son. Foolish child! Thou hast seen the breast and body of Athena, but the sun thou shalt not see again.

Therewith the mother clasped her beloved child in both her arms and, wailing the heavy plain of the mournful nightingale, led him away. And the goddess Athena pitied her comrade and spake to her and said: "Noble lady, take back all the words that thou hast spoken in anger. It is not I that made thy child blind. But the laws of Cronius [Zeus] order thus: Whosoever shall behold any of the immortals, when the god himself chooses not, at a heavy price shall he behold. Noble lady, the thing that is done can no more be taken back, since thus the thread of the Fates span when thou didst bear him from the first. Therefore, O comrade, lament not, for to this thy son—for thy sake—shall remain many other honours from me. For I will make him a seer to be sung of men hereafter, yea, more excellent than any other. Also will I give him a great staff which shall guide his feet as he hath need, and I will give him a long term of life. And he only, when he dies, shall walk among the dead having understanding, honoured of the great Leader of Peoples."

So she spake and bowed her head. That word is fulfilled over which Pallas bows, since to Athena only among his daughters hath Zeus granted that she should win all things that belong to her sire, O companions of the Bath, and no mother bare that goddess, but the head of Zeus. The head of Zeus bows not in falsehood, and in falsehood his daughter hath no part.

Now comes Athena in very deed. O maidens, whose task it is, receive ye the goddess with pious greeting and with prayer, and with the voice of thanksgiving. Hail, goddess, and have thou Inachian Argos in thy keeping! Hail when thou drivest forth thy steeds, and home again mayst thou drive them with joy, and do thou preserve all the estate of the Danaans.

—tr. A.W. Mair, 1921

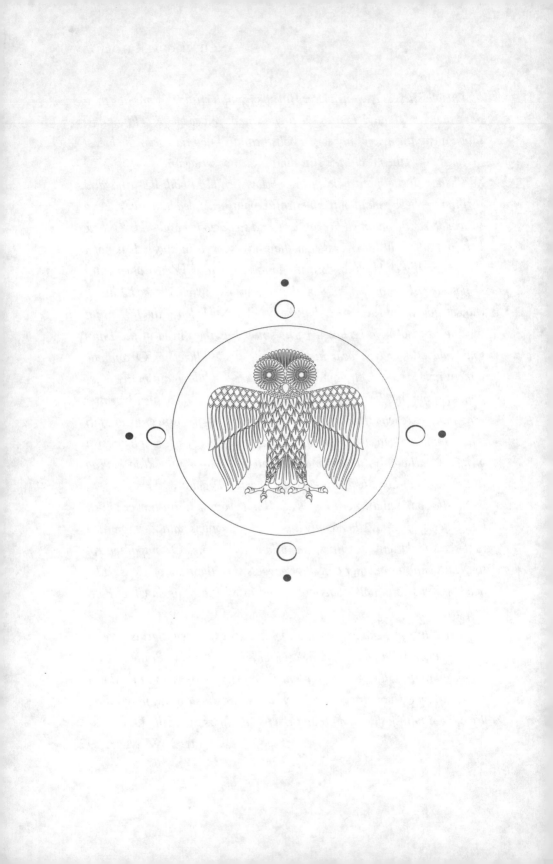

Skiraphorion
June

The major festival this month is the Skira for Demeter, which is closely related to the Thesmophoria in the fall. There is also a festival for Athena and two for Zeus. The rite for Athena at the beginning of the month is the Arrephoria, which is a secret ritual carried out by two specially chosen girls rather than a public festival. The first festival for Zeus is the Dipolieia, a curious proceeding where the weapon used to sacrifice a bull is put on trial for murder. This honors Zeus Polieus—Zeus of the City or Protector of the City. The second comes on the last day of the month—which is also the last day of the year. This ritual is for Zeus Soter—Zeus the Savior—a form of the God who delivers his suppliants from harm.

There are two sacrifices in smaller Attic towns this month, once in Erchia and one in Marathon. The sacrifice at Marathon is to the Tritopatores, the community ancestors. The Erchian sacrifice on the same date as the Arrephoria in Athens is offered to Poseidon, both Athena and Zeus in their guises as protectors of the city (Polias and Polieus respectively) and to Kourotrophos—the one who raises children. It also honors Pandrosos, one of the daughters of Cecrops, the half-snake mythical founding king of Athens. She and her two sisters were entrusted by Athena with the care of the baby Erectheus (later a great king of the city.) When they looked into his basket—in defiance of the instructions of the Goddess—they saw a snake and two of the three threw themselves off the Acropolis to their deaths. All the figures honored in this sacrifice have a role in either the early founding myths of Athens or in the ongoing maintenance of the state, and figure in the myth enacted in the Arrephoria. Take note of the following dates:

3rd of the month: Arrephoria, an Athenian festival for Athena

3rd of the month: sacrifice to Kourotrophos, Athena Polias, Aglauros, Zeus Polieus, Poseidon and Pandrosos in the Attic town of Erchia

11th of the month: sacrifice to the Tritopatores in the Attic town of Marathon

12th of the month: Skira, an Attic festival for Demeter

14th of the month: Dipolieia, an Athenian festival in honor of Zeus Polieus

30th of the month: Diisoteria, an Attic festival for Zeus Soter in Piraeus

30th of the month: sacrifice to Zeus Soter in Athens

Arrephoria

Each year, two young girls seven years of age were chosen to serve Athena and live on the Acropolis near the Erectheion temple. They are called the arrephoroi. On the day of the Arrephoria, these girls are directed in a secret ritual by the priestess of Athena. On the night of their last day of service to the Goddess, the girls dress in white gowns and the priestess gives them baskets containing secret, sacred objects. The nature of the objects is not known in modern times and was not known by the girls or the priestess in ancient times, either. The arrephoroi carried these baskets on their heads down into a natural cavern within the sanctuary of Aphrodite in the Gardens. The steps there date to the Bronze Age, so the ritual may have been quite ancient. They leave the baskets there in the shrine of Aphrodite and Eros and bring something back wrapped in a veil. When they delivered this object to the priestess on the Acropolis, the girls' duties had been completed and they returned to their families to live in their homes. Any gold jewelry they wore during the rite was consecrated to the Goddess.

The ritual itself is obscure—intentionally so, as the participants did not know what they carried—but it relates to the story of the three daughters of king Cecrops—Aglauros, Herse and Pandrosos. When Hephaestos failed to rape Athena, she wiped his seed from her thigh with a bit of wool and threw it to the Earth, where it conceived the child Erectheos who was birthed from the very rock of the Acropolis. The Goddess gave the baby to the daughters of the king in a basket, asking them to keep it for a little while she was away. She told them not to look into it but they did and saw a snake lurking within. Whether the snake was the child, a companion of the child or a threat to the child is uncertain. The girls were so terrified that two of them threw themselves off the Acropolis, with Pandrosos most likely the one who retained her wits. Erectheos himself grew to become a great man and he succeeded Cecrops to the kingship and was honored alongside Cecrops in the Erectheion temple on the Acropolis in classical times. Athena gave to Pandrosos a sacred precinct on the Acropolis, near the olive tree which Athena gave to the city to win it in her contest with Poseidon. The name of Pandrosos means "dew" and she was responsible for tending the tree, which required dew to thrive.

Herse's name also means "dew" and the time of year of the Arrephoria is at the beginning of the time when olives ripen, when a few months of dew are required for a good crop. Perhaps the girls are bringing dew up from a well in an act of sympathetic magic. It could also be an agricultural (or general) fertility rite, as the snake in the myth along with the subterranean journey to the shrine of Aphrodite and Eros have a phallic tone—they could be descending with snakes and returning with babies (or models of these items.) Less likely given the girls' young age, perhaps it symbolized releasing the maidens from the service of the virgin Goddess to Eros, in anticipation of their future marriages. The two girls living a year in service of the Goddess may represent two who died because they didn't follow her orders. By carrying the baskets without looking inside them, the arrephoroi re-enacted a corrected version of the story in which Athena gives the girls a basket and the contents remain hidden. Whatever symbolism was at play in ancient times, the rite was never meant to revealed, even to those undergoing it, a theme that permeates its myth as well.

Skira

In high summer the Athenians celebrated the Skira—also called the Skiraphoria. This was a festival of Demeter or of Demeter and Persephone or of Demeter and Athena. This day may originally have had several holidays that were combined into a single day with several distinct sets of rituals: a procession towards Eleusis, a footrace and a secret ritual held by women in Athens. Sex was taboo on this day and married women ate garlic at the beginning of the Skira to discourage their husbands from coming too close to them.

One part of the festival was a procession from the Acropolis towards Eleusis, stopping partway at a place called *Skiron*, just before the river Kephisos. Athena was venerated as Athena Skiras—a name she took from the white color of the clay there, which Theseus used to shape her statue. In the procession, the priestess of Athena Polias, the priest of Poseidon and the priest of Helios walk together, sharing a special white shade called a skiron to shield them from unforgiving summer Sun. This canopy was carried by the ancient Eteoboutadai family that supplied the priesthoods of both Athena and Poseidon.

There is no other evidence of a cult of Helios in classical Athens, so he may have had a priesthood just for this specific ritual. The descriptions of this festival are from a late period, so it could also be a reference to Apollon, as he was frequently syncretized as a Sun God after the classical era. Because the Eteoboutadai had bronze age roots and the Mycenaeans venerated the Sun, it is possible that this family upheld an ancient tradition of veneration of Helios as they did for Athena and Poseidon. As Helios was the traditional witness to oaths, it could also be that this

Helios personifying noon by Anton Raphael Mengs

day was a day for renewing the oaths that allowed the cults of Athena in Athens and Demeter in Eleusis to coexist and seamlessly intertwine. If that were the case, Poseidon's priest would have been present because he was also worshipped at Eleusis and the Eumolpidae family who provided the priesthood of the Great Mysteries counted the God as an ancestor.

This site of this ritual was used at another time of year for ritual plowing. The specific actions that happened at the shrine during the Skira were not recorded, but the whole was considered a fertility ritual to bless the crops and the harvest. This is the time of grain cutting and also when grape vines first begin to set fruit. To honor that aspect of the season there was a race of young men carrying grape vines. The prize was a mixture of the various seasonal agricultural products: olive oil, wine, honey, cheese and grain. Most was this was offered to Athena Skiras, with the only other share set aside for the victor.

On the same day, the women of the city enacted a secret ritual in the caves of the Thesmophoria. Piglets were sacrificed in honor of Demeter and then placed in the caves which were sacred to the Two Goddesses. The legend went that when Hades kidnapped Persephone, a swineherd named Eubouleus was grazing his pigs in the area. When the chariot of Hades returned beneath the Earth with Persephone, the pigs fell into the chasm as well, and so placing pigs in caves marks the anniversary of the kidnapping. The pigs set in caverns at the Skira may have been the same ones whose remains would be brought out in the fall at the Thesmophoria and spread on the fields when the winter wheat and barley were sown.

Excerpt from the Homeric Hymn to Helios

As he rides in his chariot, he shines upon men and deathless gods, and piercingly he gazes with his eyes from his golden helmet. Bright rays beam dazzlingly from him, and his bright locks streaming from the temples of his head gracefully enclose his far-seen face: a rich, fine-spun garment glows upon his body and flutters in the wind: and stallions carry him. Then, when he has stayed his golden-yoked chariot and horses, he rests there upon the highest point of heaven, until he marvelously drives them down again through heaven to Ocean.

Hail to you, lord! Freely bestow on me substance that cheers the heart.

—tr. Hugh Evelyn-White, 1914

Dipolieia

The tale goes that in the early days of Athens, the people gathered and set food offerings on the altar of Zeus Polieus, Zeus of the City. A farmer's ox, the man's partner in all his labor in the fields, wandered over and ate one of the cakes. To steal from the Gods was a great crime that could incur their wrath. To appease them, the priest of Zeus killed the ox in the very first blood sacrifice. But blood demands blood, and the guilt of such slaughter was great.

The annual festival of Diploieia was also called Bouphonia—the ox-slaying. The people gathered on the Acropolis at the sacred precinct of Zeus Polieus, where there was a small temple and in the open air a bronze table, as in the old Mycenaean style of sacrifice. One priest placed wheat, barley and cakes on this altar, while others drove oxen around and around it. Finally one ox would eat from the offerings, and a priest would immediately strike it with a blow from a pole-axe—a double-headed axe common in Mycenaean and Minoan imagery. That priest ran from the sanctuary, and the throat of the ox was cut with a knife.

At other sacrifices, animals were sometimes made to nod or to shake their heads to signal their consent, so perhaps the ox was volunteering for the slaughter when it profaned the offerings to the God who guards the city. Nevertheless, blood-guilt cannot go unpunished. But who bears the guilt? A weapon must be sharpened, and the stone must be wet, so the girls who carried the water that wet the stone that sharpened the axe must be guilty. But the girls denied having any fault and said the blame lay with the men who sharpened the axe. They denied fault, too, and blamed the man who struck the ox on the head. He in turn blamed the man who killed the victim by slitting its throat.

That man denied that he had killed the ox—it was the axe that cut the throat! So the axe itself was put on trial. Still bloody, its guilt was evident and it was sentenced to death for its crime. This was carried out by drowning—the axe was thrown in the sea.

The ox was cooked and eaten and after the feast it was skinned. Then it was immediately stuffed and set up to resemble a living animal, yoked to a plow, in accordance with an oracle from Delphi.

There is another tale behind the first blood sacrifice reenacted at the Bouphonia as well. When the Athenians were choosing whether to have Athena or Poseidon as ruler of the city, the citizens voted on which God they preferred. Athena was worried that it might be close and entreated her father for his support. Zeus voted for Athena —in exchange for the bribe of receiving the first sacrifice.

Zeus enthroned

Diisoteria

The Athenian year ended with two simultaneous events in honor of Zeus Soter—Zeus the Savior. There was a public festival in Piraeus, the port of Athens. The temple there was dedicated to Zeus Soter along with Athena Soteira—Athena the savior. This was a late period festival, and may have been inspired by the Gods' protection of Athens during the Persian Wars or at some other significant moment.

The procession was led by the maiden with a basket on her head, the sacrificial weapon hidden by the barley within. She was

Ruins of the Temple of Olympian Zeus

followed by epheboi—soldiers in training and a large number of bulls. When they arrived at the temple, these were sacrificed not just to the two saviors of the city, but to many Gods.

On the same day—the last day of both the month and the year—the government officials gathered in the agora in Athens before the statue of Zeus. They sacrificed to him and changed their posts, some stepping down and others taking their oaths of office before the God.

Hymn to Zeus from Agamemnon by Aeschylus

Zeus, whoever he may be—if by this name it pleases him to be invoked, by this name I call to him—as I weigh all things in the balance, I have nothing to compare save Zeus" if in truth I must cast aside this vain burden from my heart.

He who once was mighty, swelling with insolence for every fight, he shall not even be named as having ever existed; and he who arose later, he has met his overthrower and is past and gone. But whoever willingly sings a victory song for Zeus, he shall gain wisdom altogether.

Zeus, who sets mortals on the path to understanding, Zeus, who has established as a fixed law that wisdom comes by suffering. But even as trouble, bringing memory of pain, drips over the mind in sleep, so wisdom comes to men, whether they want it or not. Harsh, it seems to me, is the grace of gods enthroned upon their awful seats.

–tr. Herbert Weir Smyth, 1926

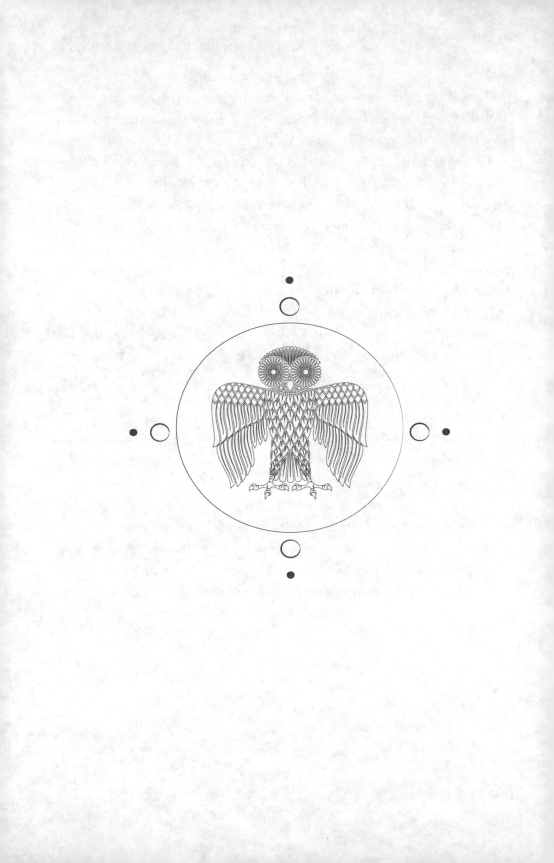

Periodic Festivals & Festivals of Unknown Date

There are a large number of sacrifices recorded to many Gods and heroes as well as references to festivals whose dates and details are not known. Additionally, some festivals occurred regularly but not annually. These included the series of four Pan-Hellenic games that drew the best athletes from all the Greek cities to compete. Take note of the following periodic festivals:

Asclepieia—a festival for the healing God held every four years at his main sanctuary at Epidauros, nine days after the Isthmian Games. Participants underwent rituals of spiritual cleansing and there were athletic and musical contests and feasting in addition to sacrifices to Asclepius.

Daidala—a festival for Hera held on Mount Cithaeron every 59 years

Daphnephoria—a Theban festival for Apollon held every nine years

Eleutheria—a festival for Zeus in Plataea every four years to thank the Gods for assistance defeating the Persians at the battle of Plataea

Heraea—a festival at Argos held every fourth year for Hera The procession included the priestess of Hera riding an ox-drawn chariot There was a large sacrifice—a hecatomb—and athletic games for which the prize was a large bronze shield.

Isthmian Games—Pan-Hellenic Games held every two years at Corinth in honor of Poseidon

Nemean Games—Pan-Hellenic Games held every two years at Nemea in honor of Zeus

Olympic Games—Pan-Hellenic Games held every four years at Olympia in honor of Zeus

Pythian Games—Pan-Hellenic Games held every four years at Delphi in honor of Apollon

Take note of the following festivals of uncertain date:

Arkteia—an Attic festival for Artemis

Brauronia—an Attic festival for Artemis

Epikleidia—an Athenian festival for Demeter

Galaxia—an Athenian festival for the mother of the Gods, featuring barley cooked in milk

Hephaisteia—an Athenian festival for Hephaistos with a torch race. The sacrifice included the raising up overhead of bulls as they were slaughtered. The festival also involved the *epheboi*—soldiers in training.

Hyacinthia—an early summer Spartan festival honoring Hyacinthus, the lover of Apollon

Laphria—a festival for Artemis in Patras

Lycaea—a festival of Zeus on Mount Lycaeus. The region was considered backwards to the point of barbarism and dark rumors of human sacrifice surrounded the festival.

Promethia—an Athenian festival for Prometheus involving a torch race

Sacrifice to the Dioscuri—the Athenians sacrificed three different kinds of animals to the Dioscuri

Sacrifice and Festival of Pan—an Athenian occasion honoring the God for his aid at the battle of Marathon

Theoxenia—a banquet for the Gods in Delphi. One of the months in Delphi takes its name from this festival

Festival of Artemis Orthia—a Spartan festival for the Goddess under the epithet Orthia, a name associated with an earlier

Goddess. Her sacred precinct in Sparta had many masks and tens of thousands of votive offerings. At her festival, cheese was placed on the altar. Soldiers in training had to attempt to steal it and were whipped if caught.

Pan-Hellenic Games

Greek festivals are notably competitive. Music, plays, poetry, crafts and many other skills at which true excellence could be attained and recognized were sacralized in festival competitions—*agones*. The ones that endure to the modern day are the athletic contests. While it might be easy to imagine that physical competitions originated as war games—they did display the skills of the soldier—these contests arose out of funeral rites. The very first athletic competition in literature is the funeral games for Patroclus in the *Iliad* and they occur in historical sources from the 6th century BCE onwards. Funeral competitions honored

the dead by offering the very best from the living, and prizes were awarded just as at later games.

The funeral of Patroclus included events similar to those held at the Olympic Games in the classical period. Held in honor of Zeus at Olympia, these ancient games also honored Pelops, a local hero. These were religious rituals rather than secular occasions, and competitors were expected to maintain an unusually strict level of ritual purity, abstaining from both sex and meat for a month beforehand. Pelops received offerings before a hecatomb of oxen were sacrificed to Zeus on the great altar, which was made entirely of compacted ash from sacrifices. It rose in a cone shape, and over the more than ten centuries during which it was used, it eventually attained a height of nearly 23 feet. The original and most prestigious event at the games was a footrace for the honor of lighting the fire on this altar. The early races and wrestling matches only lasted one day but over time became a five-day affair with chariot races, horse races, jumping, boxing, a pentathlon and contests of men in armor and contests for boys. There was a great feast in honor of the victors, who competed for the prize of an olive wreath.

There were four major festivals of Pan-Hellenic Games, meaning that the competitors came from all over Greece and not just from the host states. The series of games was held in a fixed order over a period of four years known as an *Olympiad*. The Olympic and Pythian Games were every four years and the Isthmian and Nemean every other year, so that the order of the *periodos*—the circuit—was Olympic, Nemean, Isthmian, Pythian, Nemean and Isthmian. The Pythian Games for the God of music naturally included musical and poetic contests as well as athletic competitions similar to the Olympics, and the prize was a laurel wreath. The prize at the Isthmian Games was a wreath of dried celery, in contrast to the fresh celery that graced the brows of the Nemean victors. The Nemean Games had a larger number of events for boys than for men.

In keeping with the funerary tradition, each games honored a deceased local hero in addition to the God of the city. The Nemeian Games for Zeus at Nemea honored Archemoros, the Pythian Games of Apollon at Delphi honored the snake slain by Apollon when he claimed the site and the Isthmian Games for Poseidon at Corinth also honored Palaimon. Each set of games was supposed to have begun with the associated hero's funeral, except for the Nemean which were founded by Herakles after he killed the Nemean Lion. The Olympic Games honored Pelops in addition to Zeus.

From Pindar's Olympic Ode to Hiero of Syracuse, victor of the horse race

In thy famed courses, Pelops, rise
The Olympian glories to the skies,
And shine afar. There we behold
The stretch of manhood, strenuous, bold,
In sore fatigues, and there the strife
Of winged feet. Thrice happy he,
Who overcomes! for he shall see
Unclouded days, and taste the sweets of life.

−tr. Ambrose Philips, 1748,
spelling modernized by M. Borden

Daidala

Hera the ox-eyed Goddess has few myths that don't involve her relentless jealousy. She endlessly torments the various rivals for her husband's attention and at times can seem like a caricature of a wife. Do not mistake her for anything other than the Queen of the Gods, though—her vehemence is simply an expression of her great power. The temple of Hera at Olympia—the great sanctuary of Zeus—was older than her husband's, and her enthroned statue was older than his as well. Her name is attested in Mycenaean Linear B tablets as "E-ra," and her great temple on the island of Samos was a site of pilgrimage, with votive offerings from Egypt and the Near East as well as from the Aegean islands and mainland Greece. The guardian of sacred marriage, she was a fierce protector of home, family and moral rectitude.

There is a story that on one occasion when Hera and Zeus were arguing, the Queen of the Gods hid from her husband on Mount Cithaeron. To draw her out and stoke her ire, Zeus dressed up a wooden statue in bridal clothes. When he claimed he was going to marry the doll, Hera came out from her hiding place to assault this rival to her position. Seeing that it was a trick, she was reunited with her husband and they burned the doll together. The people of Boeotia reenacted this mythological event every 59 years at the Daidala. This name of this festival of Hera means "finely worked objects" and refers to wooden statues. They processed up Mount Cithaeron with daidala, one of which was decked out in a bridal costume. On reaching the sacred site, they sacrificed to the Gods and then built a bonfire and cast the the daidala into the flames.

Homeric Hymn to Hera

I sing of golden-throned Hera whom Rhea bare. Queen of the immortals is she, surpassing all in beauty. She is the sister and the wife of loud-thundering Zeus, the glorious one whom all the blessed throughout high Olympus reverence and honor even as Zeus who delights in thunder.

–tr. Hugh Evelyn-White, 1914

Hyacinthia

Apollon loved the Spartan youth Hyacinthus. Neglecting his temples, the God set aside his lyre and his bow and all his own pursuits to spend his days with his lover. They shared a passion for athletics, and one day they climbed a mountain together, Hyacinthus leading the way and the God scrambling behind him, carrying nets and managing their dogs. Around noon the lovers prepared to compete with the discus, taking off their clothes and rubbing their bodies with olive oil, as athletes do. Apollon had the first throw. To impress Hyacinthus he showed off his divine strength, throwing the discus so high and so far across the sky that it scattered the clouds. When it dropped back down to Earth, Hyacinthus was eager for his own turn and went out as if to catch it. But it bounced hard against the ground and then smashed into his face, killing him on the spot. As Hyacinthus' body grew pale in death, Apollon's face grew pale in grief and he lingered long, mourning the boy. He swore to remember him always in his songs and to create a flower that would bear the marks of his grief. As he lamented, purple flowers sprang up from the ground where the boy's blood had spilled, and Apollon marked their petals, "AI AI," so that they would always bear the grief of the God.

The Spartans honored Hyacinthus, the lover of the Apollon, at the Hyacinthia festival in early summer. It opened with mourning for their lost hero—there were no bright garlands, no festive hymns. There were no rich foods or heavy-laden feast tables. Part of the way through, a hymn began to make its way through the gathering and then the atmosphere became festive. Over the next several days, there was a large procession, choral performances, a great feast and—fittingly—athletic competitions.

Poem to Hyacinthus

When he beheld thy agony Phoebus was dumb. He sought every remedy, he had recourse to cunning arts, he anointed all the wound, anointed it with ambrosia and with nectar, but all remedies are powerless to heal the wounds of Fate.

Bion of Phlossa
−tr. J.M. Edmonds, 1912

Engravings of Apollo and Hyacinth by
Marcantonio Raimondi

Festival of Pan

Pan the hunter, Pan the shepherd, Pan the player on the sweet pipes, the lover so often unrequited, the wanderer on the mountaintops. The goat-hooved deity originated in Arcadia, a rough, mountainous region where local hunters would whip the God's statue if their efforts were unsuccessful. His worship spread throughout Greece and he was usually honored in natural settings such as caves. Even in the city, natural spots would be found—a small crevice under the Acropolis became his temenos in Athens.

Pan's festival in Athens featured a torch race that originated with the first marathon race—the famous race of Philippides. When word of the coming Persian attack made its way to Athens in the fall of 490 BCE, Philippides ran 150 miles from Athens to Sparta in two days to beg for aid. He then ran back to Athens and on to the battlefield at Marathon, all without stopping for food or rest. When he was crossing a mountain in the Peloponnese, Philippides heard the God Pan calling out to him. The Athenians had never established worship of Pan, but the God promised to aid them in the future as he had in the past.

The Spartans delayed sending help to Athens as they were engaged in the Karneia festival, a time at which they would not take up weapons or go to war. Athens was victorious without them, due in part to the great panic that struck the Persian troops on the battlefield, a panic that the Athenians attributed to the God Pan acting on their behalf. After the battle, Philippes ran the 26 miles from Marathon to Athens to deliver the news of victory. As soon as he delivered his message, he collapsed from exhaustion and died with the word "joy" on his lips. After the war, Athens established a sacred precinct for Pan in the cave under the Acropolis and established both sacrifices and the torch race in his honor.

Excerpted from the Homeric Hymn to Pan

Muse, tell me about Pan, the dear son of Hermes, with his goat's feet and two horns—a lover of merry noise. Through wooded glades he wanders with dancing nymphs who foot it on some sheer cliff's edge, calling upon Pan, the shepherd-god, long-haired, unkempt. He has every snowy crest and the mountain peaks and rocky crests for his domain. Hither and thither he goes through the close thicket.

Often he courses through the glistening high mountains, and often on the shouldered hills he speeds along slaying wild beasts, this keen-eyed god. Only at evening, as he returns from the chase, he sounds his note, playing sweet and low on his pipes of reed.

At that hour the clear-voiced nymphs are with him and move with nimble feet, singing by some spring of dark water, while Echo wails about the mountain-top, and the god on this side or on that of the choirs, or at times sidling into the midst, plies it nimbly with his feet. On his back he wears a spotted lynx-pelt, and he delights in high-pitched songs in a soft meadow where crocuses and sweet-smelling hyacinths bloom at random in the grass.

–tr. Hugh Evelyn-White, 1914

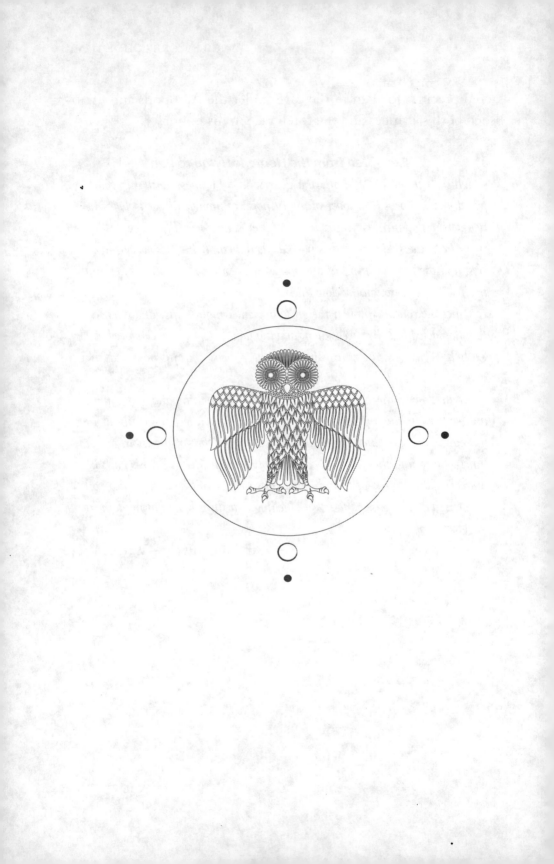

Appendices

Appendix I
Festivals by Associated Deities

Appendix II
Lunar Month Dates

Appendix I
Festivals by Associated Deities

ACHELOUS
Sacrifice to the nymphs, Achelous, Alochus, Hermes and Gaia in
Boedromion

AGLAUROS
Sacrifice to Kourotrophos, Athena Polias, Aglauros, Zeus Polias,
Poseidon and Pandrosos in Skiraphorion

ALOCHUS
Sacrifice to the nymphs, Achelous, Alochus, Hermes and Gaia in
Boedromion

APHRODITE
Aphrodisia in Hekatombaion

APOLLON
Gymnopaidia in Hekatombaion
Karneia in Metageitnion
Metageitnia in Metageitnion
Boedromia in Boedromion
Pyanepsia in Pyanepsion
Sacrifice to Apollo Apotropaeus, Apollo Nymphegetes and the
Nymphs in Gamelion
Procession to the Delphinion in Munichion
Thargelia in Thargelion
Sacrifice to Leto, Pythian Apollo, Zeus, Hermes and the Dioscuri
in Thargelion

Pythian Games, every four years
Daphnephoria, uncertain date
Hyacinthia, uncertain date
Theoxenia, uncertain date

ARTEMIS

Sacrifice to Kourotrophos, Hecate and Artemis in Metageitnion
Charisteria in Boedromion
Elaphebolia in Elaphebolion
Munichia in Munichion
Procession to the Delphinion in Munichion
Arketeia, uncertain date
Brauronia, uncertain date
Laphria, uncertain date

ASCLEPIUS

Epidauria in Boedromion
Asclepieia at Athens in Elaphebolion
Asclepieia at Epidauros, every four years

ATHENA

Panathenaia in Hekatombaion
Sacrifice to Athena by Teithras in Boedromion
Apaturia in Pyanepsion
Chalkeia in Pyanepsion
Sacrifice to Athena by Erchia in Gamelion
Kallynteria in Thargelion
Plynteria in Thargelion
Arrephoria in Skiraphorion
Skira in Skiraphorion

Sacrifice to Kourotrophos, Athena Polias, Aglauros, Zeus Polias,
Poseidon and Pandrosos in Skiraphorion

BASILE
Sacrifice to Basile in Boedromion
Bendis
Bendidia in Thargelion

THE DEAD
Genesia in Boedromion

DEMETER
Eleusinia in Metageitnion
Eleusinian Mysteries in Boedromion
Proerosia in Pyanepsion
Stenia in Pyanepsion
Thesmophoria in Pyanepsion
Plerosia in Poseideon
Haloa in Poseideon
Lesser Mysteries in Anthesterion
Skira in Skiraphorion
Epikleidia, uncertain date

DIONYSUS
Eleusinian Mysteries (as Iakchos) in Boedromion
Oschophoria in Pyanepsion
Country Dionysia in Poseideon
Haloa (as Iakchos) in Poseideon
Lenaia in Gamelion
Anthesteria in Anthesterion
Sacrifice to Dionysus in Anthesterion
City Dionysia in Elaphebolion

THE DIOSCURI

Sacrifice to the Dioscuri in Athens, uncertain date
Sacrifice to Leto, Pythian Apollo, Zeus, Hermes and the Dioscuri
   in Thargelion

EROS

Festival of Eros in Munichion

GAIA

Sacrifice to the nymphs, Achelous, Alochus, Hermes and Gaia
   in Boedromion

HECATE

Sacrifice to Kourotrophos, Hecate and Artemis in Metageitnion

HELIOS

Skira in Skiraphorion

HEPHAESTOS

Chalkeia in Pyanepsion
Hephaestia, uncertain date

HERA

Heraea, every four years
Daidala, every 59 years
Sacrifice to Hera Telchinia in Metageitnion
Gamelia in Gamelion
Sacrifice to Kourotrophos, Hera, Zeus Teleius and Poseidon
   in Gamelion

HERAKLES

Festival of Herakles in Metageitnion

HERMES

Sacrifice to the nymphs, Achelous, Alochus, Hermes and Gaia in
    Boedromion
Anthesteria in Anthesterion
Sacrifice to Leto, Pythian Apollo, Zeus, Hermes and the Dioscuri in
    Thargelion

THE HEROINES

Sacrifice to the Heroines in Metageitnion
Sacrifice to the Heroines in Pyanepsion

HYACINTHUS

Hyacinthia, uncertain date in early summer

KOUROTROPHOS

Sacrifice to Kourotrophos, Hecate and Artemis in Metageitnion
Sacrifice to Kourotrophos, Hera, Zeus Teleius and Poseidon in
    Gamelion
Sacrifice to Kourotrophos, Athena Polias, Aglauros, Zeus Polias,
    Poseidon and Pandrosos in Skiraphorion

KRONOS

Kronia in Hekatombaion
Private sacrifice to Kronos in Elaphebolion

LETO

Sacrifice to Leto, Pythian Apollo, Zeus, Hermes and the Dioscuri
    in Thargelion

LEUCASPIS
Sacrifice to Leucaspis in Munichion

MENEDEIUS
Sacrifice to Menedeius in Thargelion

THE MOTHER OF THE GODS
Galaxia, uncertain date

THE NYMPHS
Sacrifice to the nymphs, Achelous, Alochus, Hermes and Gaia in
    Boedromion
Sacrifice to Apollo Apotropaeus, Apollo Nymphegetes and the
    Nymphs in Gamelion

PAN
Sacrifice and Festival of Pan, uncertain date

PANDROSUS
Sacrifice to Kourotrophos, Athena Polias, Aglauros, Zeus Polias,
    Poseidon and Pandrosos in Skiraphorion

PERSEPHONE
Eleusinian Mysteries in Boedromion
Stenia in Pyanepsion
Thesmophoria in Pyanepsion
Haloa in Poseideon
Lesser Mysteries in Anthesterion

POSEIDON
Poseidea in Poseideon

Sacrifice to Kourotrophos, Hera, Zeus Teleius and Poseidon in
    Gamelion
Sacrifice to Kourotrophos, Athena Polias, Aglauros, Zeus Polias,
    Poseidon and Pandrosos in Skiraphorion
Isthmian Games, every two years

PROMETHEUS
Promethia, uncertain date

THESEUS
Theseia in Pyanepsion

THE TRITOPATORES
Sacrifice to the Tritopatores in Munichion
Sacrifice to the Tritopatores in Skiraphorion

THE WIND GODS
Private sacrifice to the Wind Gods in Poseideon

ZEUS
Sacrifice to Zeus Epoptes in Metageitnion
Apaturia in Pyanepsion
Pompaia in Maimakterion
Plerosia in Poseideon
sacrifice to Zeus Horios in Poseideon
Gamelia in Gamelion
sacrifice to Kourotrophos, Hera, Zeus Teleius and Poseidon
    in Gamelion
Diasia in Anthesterion
Olympieia in Munichion

Sacrifice to Leto, Pythian Apollo, Zeus, Hermes and the Dioscuri in
    Thargelion
Sacrifice to Zeus Epacrios in Thargelion
Dipolieia in Skiraphorion
Diisoteria in Skiraphorion
Sacrifice to Kourotrophos, Athena Polias, Aglauros, Zeus Polias,
    Poseidon and Pandrosos in Skiraphorion
Nemean Games, every two years
Eleutheria, every four years
Lycaea, uncertain date
Olympic Games, every four years

Appendix II
Lunar Month Dates

If you choose to calculate festival dates based on the lunar months, the dates of the New Moons are given below through 2030. To find the date of any festival, simply count the appropriate number of days from the New Moon in that month, bearing in mind that the ancient day begins at dusk rather than at midnight. For example, the Genesia festival falls on the 5th of the month of Boedromion. The first day of Boedromion is the third New Moon in the year, generally the New Moon in September because the year begins with the New Moon in July. If you were to celebrate the Genesia in the year 2026 by the lunar date, you would begin by identifying the date of the New Moon. The first sliver should be visible around 11:30 p.m. on September 10th by the modern calendar, after dusk. By the ancient reckoning, the day begins at nightfall, so the ancient date of the New Moon would actually correspond to the 11th, making September 15th the Genesia festival. In the table below, the dates have been adjusted for the Almanac's local sunset times in Newport, Rhode Island.

Because the solar year is longer than the lunar year, every third year has an intercalary (13th) month. This is listed below as a second Skiraphorion, but the festivals in Skiraphorion should not be celebrated twice. For ease of mapping onto the modern year, the dates below begin with the month of Gamelion in January. The ancient year, however, began in Hekatombaion, so the first date listed for Gamelion in 2023 is the continuation of the ancient year which began in July of 2022.

Beginning Date by Year

Ancient Month	2023	2024	2025*	2026	2027	2028*	2029	2030
Gamelion	Jan. 21	Jan. 11	Dec. 31 2024	Jan. 18	Jan. 7	Dec. 27 2027	Jan. 14	Jan. 4
Anthisterion	Feb. 20	Feb, 10	Jan. 29	Feb. 17	Feb. 6	Jan. 26	Feb. 13	Feb. 2
Elaphebolion	Mar. 21	Mar. 10	Feb. 28	Mar. 19	Mar. 8	Feb. 25	Mar. 15	Mar. 4
Munichion	April 20	Apr. 8	Mar. 29	Apr. 17	Apr. 7	Mar. 26	Apr. 13	Apr. 2
Thargelion	May 19	May 8	Apr. 27	May 16	May 6	Apr. 24	May 13	May 2
Skiraphorion	June 18	June 6	May 27	June 15	June 4	May 24	June 12	June 1
2 Skiraphorion			June 25			June 22		
Hecatombaion	July 17	July 5	July 24	July 14	July 4	July 22	July 11	June 30
Metageitnion	Aug. 16	Aug. 4	Aug. 23	Aug. 12	Aug. 2	Aug. 20	Aug. 10	July 30
Boedromion	Sept. 15	Sept. 3	Sept. 21.	Sept. 11	Aug. 31	Sept. 18	Sept. 8	Aug. 28
Pyanepsion	Oct. 14	Oct. 2	Oct. 21	Oct. 10	Sept. 30	Oct. 18	Oct. 7	Sept. 27
Maïmakterion	Nov. 13	Nov. 1	Nov. 20	Nov. 9	Oct. 29	Nov. 16	Nov. 6	Oct. 26
Poseideon	Dec. 13	Dec. 1	Dec. 20	Dec. 9	Nov. 28	Dec. 16	Dec. 5	Nov. 25

*Years with an intercalary month.

Bibliography

Aeschylus, and Oliver Taplin. *The Oresteia*. New York: Liveright Publishing Corporation, 2018.

Aristophanes. *The Frogs of Aristophanes*. Translated by Gilbert Murray. London: George Allen and Company, Ltd., 1912.

Aristophanes. *Aristophanes; with the English Translation of Benjamin Bickley Rogers: The Lysistrata, the Thesmophoriazusae, the Ecclesiazusae, the Plutus*. 1927. Reprint, Harvard University Press, 1996.

Aristotle, and Jonathan Barnes. *Complete Works of Aristotle, Volume 1: The Revised Oxford Translation*. Princeton: Princeton University Press, 2014.

Athanassakis, Apostolos N, and Benjamin M Wolkow. *The Orphic Hymns*. Baltimore: Johns Hopkins University Press, 2013.

Bodel, John, and Saul M Olyan. *Household and Family Religion in Antiquity*. John Wiley & Sons, 2012.

Burkert, Walter. *Greek Religion Archaic and Classical*. Malden, Mass. Blackwell, 2012.

Callimachus. *Callimachus, Works*. Translated by A. W. Mair. New York: William Heinemann, 1921.

Evelyn, Hugh G. *Hesiod, the Homeric Hymns and Homerica*. Cambridge: Harvard University Press, 1919.

Garland, Robert. *Daily Life of the Ancient Greeks*. Westport, Conn.: Greenwood Press, 2009.

———. "Greek and Roman Priests and Religious Personnel." Oxford Research Encyclopedia of Religion, April 5, 2016. https://doi.org/10.1093/acrefore/9780199340378.013.25.

Graf, Fritz. "Festivals in Ancient Greece and Rome." Oxford

Research Encyclopedia of Religion, May 9, 2016. https://doi. org/10.1093/acrefore/9780199340378.013.58.

Homer. The Iliad. Translated by Emily Wilson. New York: W. W. Norton & Company, 2023.

———. *The Iliad* with an English Translation. Translated by A.T. Murray. Vol. 1 and 2. Cambridge, MA: Harvard University Press, 1924.

———. *The Odyssey*. Translated by Emily Wilson. New York: W.W. Norton and Company, 2018.

———. *The Odyssey: Rendered into English Prose for the Use of Those Who Cannot Read the Original*. Translated by Samuel L. Butler. London, 1900.

Hornblower, Simon, Antony Spawforth, and Esther Eidinow. *The Oxford Classical Dictionary*. 4th ed. Oxford: Oxford University Press, 2012.

J Rasmus Brandt, and Jon W Iddeng. *Greek and Roman Festivals: Content, Meaning, and Practice*. Oxford: Oxford University Press, 2012.

Jenny Strauss Clay, and Andrew Faulkner. "Religion in the Homeric Hymns." Oxford Research Encyclopedia of Religion, November 22, 2022. https://doi.org/10.1093/acrefore/9780199340378.013.709.

Joan Breton Connelly. *Portrait of a Priestess: Women and Ritual in Ancient Greece*. Princeton, N.J.: Princeton University Press, 2010.

Kinzl, Konrad H. A *Companion to the Classical Greek World*. Malden, Ma: Blackwell Pub, 2006.

Lefkowitz, Mary R, and James S Romm. *The Greek Plays: Sixteen Plays by Aeschylus, Sophocles, and Euripides*. New York: The Modern Library, 2017.

McClure, Laura. "Women in Classical Greek Religion." Oxford Research Encyclopedia of Religion, July 30, 2018. https://doi. org/10.1093/acrefore/9780199340378.013.256.

Ovid. *The Metamorphoses of Ovid*. Translated by Mary M Innes. New York: Penguin Books, 1993.

Parke, H.W. *Festivals of the Athenians*. Ithaca, N.Y Cornell Univ. Press, 1994.

Parker, Robert. *Athenian Religion: A History*. Oxford: Clarendon Press; New York, 1997.

Paton, W.R. *The Greek Anthology*. London: W. Heinemann, 1916.

Plato, C J Emlyn-Jones, and William Preddy. *Plato*. Cambridge, Massachusetts: Harvard University Press, 2013.

Rayor, Diane J. *The Homeric Hymns*. Berkeley: University of California Press, 2014.

Sappho, and Mary Barnard. *Sappho: A New Translation*. Berkeley: University of California Press, 2019.

Sappho, and Edwin Marion Cox. *The Poems of Sappho: With Historical & Critical Notes, Translations, and a Bibliography*. London: Williams & Norgate ; New York, 1925.

Simon, Erika. *Festivals of Attica: An Archaeological Commentary*. Madison, Wis.; London: University of Wisconsin Press, 1983.

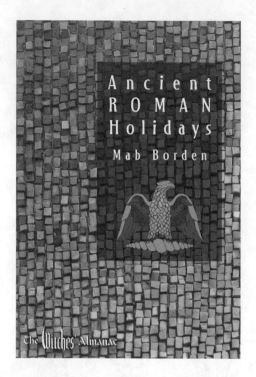

Ancient Roman Holidays by Mab Borden immerses readers in the sacred days, months and seasons of ancient Rome. Renowned for meticulous research and vivid descriptions, Borden unveils detailed accounts of revered deities and their ceremonial customs, emphasizes the profound significance of each. The book explains the ancient Roman calendar, detailing religious ritual activity and includes appendices that provide additional depth to the material presented in the book. Exploring festivals dedicated to Gods like Jupiter, Minerva and Bacchus, readers witness solemn processions and joyous celebrations. *Ancient Roman Holidays* invites readers to rediscover the beauty of these observances, revealing the traditions shaping the Roman calendar and immersing them in the vibrant tapestry of Roman spirituality and the sacred rhythms of life.

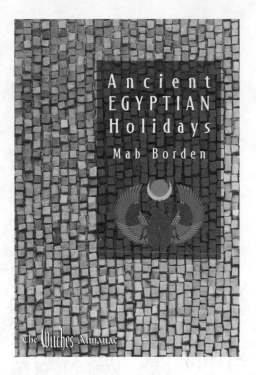

Ancient Egyptian Holidays, part of the Ancient Holidays series by Mab Borden, explores the intricate relationship between religious observances, agricultural practices and the sacred calendar of the Ancient Egyptians. It vividly portrays the cycles of sowing, cultivation and harvesting intertwined with deity worship, from the Festival of the Nile Inundation to the Feast of Opet. This book unveils the profound connection between ancient Egyptians' spiritual beliefs and agricultural livelihood, offering readers a rich mosaic of cultural traditions and rituals marking each month and season. Borden, known for meticulous research and vivid descriptions, skillfully brings these celebrations to life, inviting readers to reflect on their own spiritual connections to nature. It is an essential companion for those seeking a deeper understanding of ancient Egyptian civilization and its wisdom.

Come visit us at the
Witches' Almanac website

www.TheWitchesAlmanac.com

Aradia
Gospel of the Witches
Charles Godfrey Leland

ARADIA IS THE FIRST work in English in which witchcraft is portrayed as an underground old religion, surviving in secret from ancient Pagan times.

- Used as a core text by many modern Neo-Pagans.
- Foundation material containing traditional witchcraft practices
- This special edition features appreciations by such authors as Paul Huson, Raven Grimassi, Judika Illes, Michael Howard, Christopher Penczak, Myth Woodling, Christina Oakley Harrington, Patricia Della-Piana, Jimahl di Fiosa and Donald Weiser. A beautiful and compelling work, this edition is an up to date format, while keeping the text unchanged. 172 pages $16.95

The ABC of Magic Charms
Elizabeth Pepper

Mankind has sought protection from mysterious forces beyond mortal control. Humans have sought the help of animal, mineral, vegetable. The enlarged edition of *Magic Charms from A to Z*, guides us in calling on these forces. $12.95

The Little Book of Magical Creatures
Elizabeth Pepper and Barbara Stacy

AN UPDATE of the classic *Magical Creatures*, featuring Animals Tame, Animals Wild, Animals Fabulous—plus an added section of enchanting animal myths from other times, other places. *A must for all animal lovers.* $12.95

The Witchcraft of Dame Darrel of York
Charles Godfrey Leland, Introduction by Robert Mathiesen

A beautifully reproduced facsimile of the illuminated manuscript shedding light on the basis for a modern practice. A treasured by those practicing Pagans, as well as scholars.   Standard Hardcover $65.00 or Exclusive full leather bound, numbered and slipcased edition $145.00

DAME FORTUNE'S WHEEL TAROT: A PICTORIAL KEY
Paul Huson

Based upon Paul Huson's research in *Mystical Origins of the Tarot, Dame Fortune's Wheel Tarot* illustrates for the first time the earliest, traditional Tarot card interpretations as collected in the 1700s by Jean-Baptiste Alliette. In addition to detailed descriptions, full color reproductions of Huson's original designs for all 79 cards.

WITCHES ALL

A Treasury from past editions, is a collection from *The Witches' Almanac* publications of the past. Arranged by topics, the book, like the popular almanacs, is thought provoking and often spurs the reader on to a tangent leading to even greater discovery. It's perfect for study or casual reading,

GREEK GODS IN LOVE

Barbara Stacy casts a marvelously original eye on the beloved stories of Greek deities, replete with amorous oddities and escapades. We relish these tales in all their splendor and antic humor, and offer an inspired storyteller's fresh version of the old, old mythical magic.

MAGIC CHARMS FROM A TO Z

A treasury of amulets, talismans, fetishes and other lucky objects compiled by the staff of *The Witches' Almanac*. An invaluable guide for all who respond to the call of mystery and enchantment.

LOVE CHARMS

Love has many forms, many aspects. Ceremonies performed in witchcraft celebrate the joy and the blessings of love. Here is a collection of love charms to use now and ever after.

MAGICAL CREATURES

Mystic tradition grants pride of place to many members of the animal kingdom. Some share our life. Others live wild and free. Still others never lived at all, springing instead from the remarkable power of human imagination.

CELTIC TREE MAGIC

Robert Graves in *The White Goddess* writes of the significance of trees in the old Celtic lore. *Celtic Tree Magic* is an investigation of the sacred trees in the remarkable Beth-Luis-Nion alphabet and their role in folklore, poetry and mysticism.

MOON LORE

As both the largest and the brightest object in the night sky, and the only one to appear in phases, the Moon has been a rich source of myth for as long as there have been mythmakers.

MAGIC SPELLS
AND INCANTATIONS

Words have magic power. Their sound, spoken or sung, has ever been a part of mystic ritual. From ancient Egypt to the present, those who practice the art of enchantment have drawn inspiration from a treasury of thoughts and themes passed down through the ages.

LOVE FEASTS

Creating meals to share with the one you love can be a sacred ceremony in itself. With the Witch in mind, culinary adept Christine Fox offers magical menus and recipes for every month in the year.

RANDOM RECOLLECTIONS
III, IV

Pages culled from the original (no longer available) issues of *The Witches' Almanac,* published annually throughout the 1970s, are now available in a series of tasteful booklets. A treasure for those who missed us the first time around, keepsakes for those who remember.